Awakening
of the
Celt

Awakening

of the

Celt

DAVID J CONWAY

Library of Congress Control Number: 2016921493
ISBN: Hardcover   978-1-7960-0100-6
               Softcover   978-1-7960-0099-3
               eBook   978-1-7960-0098-6

Print information available on the last page.

Rev. date: 03/08/2019

To order additional copies of this book, contact:
Xlibris
1-800-455-039
www.Xlibris.com.au
Orders@Xlibris.com.au
792641

CONTENTS

DEDICATION

I dedicate this book to a Silent Warrior. He wasn't just my best friend's younger brother – but I always saw him in the same light. His name is Dermot (Dermo). Passed away in his sleep & his best friend Darragh (4D) – another Legend I luckily had the pleasure of many sessions with – passed away soon after.

Because we lost these two Legends and countless more – I was put in a position to write this book in the hope that we don't lose any more.

The Irish are one of the longest colonised peoples in the world but also one of the most resilient. They have turned this negative into a positive and assisted by inspiring many other people to stand up for themselves and reclaim their dignity.

Introduction

We need to pave the way for a better future for our children. We have no idea what the future holds until we understand our past. Our history has been stolen, manipulated and we have been treated like 'mushrooms' - 'kept in the dark and fed shit.'

Telling the truth, is not just a rebellion, it's an act of revolution. So think carefully when you speak it because the truth is a weapon. Finding the truth is more than a search for information, its an excavation of the self and we must keep going no matter where it takes us, as nothing can stay hidden forever!

My daughter of 7 years of age said to me the other day 'Never see a need without doing something about it.'

She's my inspiration, my angel, full of empathy and compassion – and this book, along with this Trilogy is the outcome.

To all my Irish friends, this is our story of Éire and each chapter can open up volumes of Irish stories and experiences, for this short book is a pointer to our story. Without understanding our past, we cannot make positive choices or come up with solutions for Éire's future. Thank you for reading.

CHAPTER I

The Celtic People

Ireland is a country that consists of a race of people called the Celts. A knowledgeable population of people that for over 25,000 years, lived all over Europe.

The exact origin of the Celts seems to be debatable, they traveled a lot, but they settled in Ireland and many parts of Europe after the ice age retreated 10,000 years ago.

They were very crafted people that brought knowledge and wisdom and Gold bracelets to what we call Europe today.

Also, the Irish word for Gold is Elán. It means awareness, consciousness, compassion, wisdom, knowledge, and purity. This word Elán was translated into the word Gold. So when you look into history, the Celts brought Gold bracelets and jewellery all around Europe.

The Celtic people are described as influential people, they were at one with nature, lovers of adventure and freedom, they made arts, music, and poetry, they were incredibly creative, proud and also held within - profound wisdom of mother earth, farming, the stars and sun which is all evident as we look into the structures and land of our country. Many stories were written, stories that the elders told their kids and one of these stories that's recognised around the world is the Leprechaun and the Pot of Gold. (Elán)

The only problem with the Celts all over Europe, sharing wisdom and teaching people how to be creative and live in harmony with the earth, energised and rejuvenated by the Sun, was another group called the Romans. The Romans wanted to control Europe, with a centralised power of control. They never gave up on this idea and ideas can live forever.

Many battles took place, and the Celts won those battles each time in history as far back as our story goes with the Romans.

The Celtic people would not have been in favour of any centralised authority. They were lovers of freedom, full of creativity and were philosophers, and spent their time being creative on many levels.

The Romans could not beat the Celts. The Celtic people could have taken over the Roman Empire, quite easily. But they were not interested in taking over powers, countries and killing innocent people, it is not what a civilised, compassionate race of people do but they were strong enough to defend themselves against the battles that took place against the Romans for a very long time and even till this day, still not taken over. The Celts are the resistance.

The Roman Empire grew in the first century and on the 1st century, the Celts settled permanently in Ireland (Éire), Wales (Cymru), Scotland (Alba), the Isle of Man (Celtic fringe), Cornwall (Kernow), Brittany (Breizh), which is now part of France and Galicia, which is North West Spain.

All were traveling by boat to see one another, trade, educate, tell stories and have the craic. They were a very vibrant race of people, and dealt with all the emotions, love and sadness and happiness, sexuality and life and death and were synchronous with all the seasons. Great craic was had with the 7 Celtic Nations and Ireland being the heart of all it, surrounded by protection from the other Celtic Nations.

Galicia is a fantastic place where they learn their traditional Celtic dancing in their youth, and it's the same dance as the Irish dancing – the only difference is the arms are held out, instead of, by our sides - Celtic Legends!

There are still Celtic pieces of evidence and structures in places around Europe, but most of the Celtic languages died out in those places unlike the 7 Celtic Nations above, where to this day, still Celtic language is recorded and even spoken in some parts.

There are many stories that the Celts originated in Ireland, but also many stories of the Celts being part of many countries all over Europe with the same language, skills, and beliefs. It was as though there was a big network going on, and history is not sure exactly how, as the history of the Celts sailing around from Celtic nations was removed from British history books and Irish Legend Columbanus's name replaced with Columbus in the new history books, by the Brits as being one of the first to have sailed a boat!

The Irish sailed and even settled in Canada in the year 600 well before the Brits took over. There is lot of evidence to support that lots of Irish people went to Canada and Greenland and this is known in parts of Canada and also taught in the schools in this latest generation in this 21st Century.

With regards to history, what we do know is, the Irish today are descendants of the Celts. The Celts built New Grange in Meath – Ireland 3200BC, which is older than the Egyptian pyramids and 1000 years older than Stonehenge. This spot is the Heart of the Celtic Nations and also the reason for hundreds of years of damaging and challenging history from the two Empires.

There are many sites in Ireland; also there are tall round towers that early Christian monks built as a look out from the invading Vikings of the 8th & 9th Century.

New Grange or Sí an Bhrú as it was once known, captures a ray from the rising Sun of the winter solstice on December 21st. 5,200 years old, the passageway is 19 meters long – leads to a chamber with 3 recesses. It's in the design of a crucifix, this is our Celtic Cross!

It was rediscovered as a tomb in 1699. The excavations of our New Grange was carried out in 1962 - 1975 by Professor MJ O'Kelly. On December 21, 1967, he was the first person to see the winter solstice display at New Grange in thousands of years.

From December 19 - 23, a narrow beam of light penetrates the roof-box and reaches the floor of the entrance, and gradually extends to the rear of the chamber.

From the Northern Hemisphere. From the perspective of Ireland, most importantly from the standpoint of New Grange. In the winter season, the Sun, as always - rises from the east and goes down in the west, but due to the Earths axis, these days are the shortest days and longest nights in Ireland and the Sun appears to be walking on water as it only Rises to those levels, on the shortest days.

On the third day, the Sun Rose! On the third day being the 21st December at 8:58am, as the Sun shines in each day from the 19th till the 23rd but on the 3rd day, it Rose.

From December 19th to 23rd, at dawn, on the mornings surrounding the solstice, a narrow beam of light enters the 62 - foot long passage and lights the floor. It moves along the ground, from the window box until it illuminates the rear chamber which consists of 3 recesses, making the whole area light up in a Cross which is our Celtic Cross, the very foundation of our Irish heritage, our divine right to be Irish and one of our ancestors masterpieces, this is our culture!

This event lasts for 17 minutes, beginning around 8:58am but over 5000 years we are loosing out on 4 minutes of the light show due to a slight change in the Earths axis.

The entrance is made out of quartz, mostly white quartz, which is a rock, found in the Earth. Mind you, there's a massive amount of work involved, creating this entrance out of quartz rock found in the Earth. Our ancestor's blood, sweat, and tears went into creating this magnificent structure. Rose quartz is a gentle stone that is often associated with unconditional love. People use Rose Quartz to help access self-love, express buried emotions, promote forgiveness and transmute pain into love. While, white quartz is associated with connection to the source, the inward core of all existence.

The excavator's daughter who experienced the solstice at New Grange the following year said, "Suddenly this shaft of light came into the chamber and hit the back wall. I remember being quietly moved - it was like someone was speaking to you from thousands of years before. I see it as a picture before my inner eye - it was a golden light".

This is our Celtic Cross, our divine heritage, our power of connection to source - it is the heart and soul of Ireland and the Foundation of Irish culture!

The Swirls on the rock at the front are Triads. The real interpretation of the Triad, is for the individual, as a three part being. It was translated into religion as separate from ourselves, the Father, Son and the Holy Ghost and we lost its real meaning.

Bringing this knowledge back to its core, it is the spirit within us that gives inspiration, the mind that produces the thought, developing into the idea and the body that fulfils that idea giving us the experience, then completes the full circle as the spirit has then experienced what it first inspired.

The Triad is Consciousness, mind and body, it is inspiration, thought and experience. Father is the mind, Son is the experience produced by the body and holy ghost is our inner consciousness that knows all and judges nothing, and resides in each individual. The white quartz surrounding our New grange is to connect us to source in order to be inspired in the first place. New Grange is the birth place of legends and re-birthing can occur during any return visit, for its the quartz stones themselves that connects our awareness to source, that gives the inspiration, produces the thought in the mind, which is the foundation of the idea, whereas the body experiences that idea throughout the life lived. The Swirls on the rocks are a deeper understanding than any language, explaining what your in for, entering this magnificent creation.

Many individuals live - place their energy, their consciousness in their minds, some live soulfully in their spirits, some live for the experiences. The aim of the game is to have the three aspects, the three states of being, mind body and spirit, emerged as One, awakened together as One, in the present moment and each moment onwards, that my friends is the Christ Consciousness, that many before us, have attained and unfortunately those in power, that do not want us to attain by restricting us with false beliefs.

New Grange is believed to be built 600 years before the Great Pyramids and more than 1000 years before Stonehenge according to researchers, but other historians think that New Grange is much older than that.

New Grange is part of a large complex of monuments built along a bend of the River Boyne known collectivity as Brú na Bóinne, which means Palace of the Boyne.

The other two are Knowth (the largest) and Dowth, and throughout the region, there are as many as 35 smaller passage tombs and many other sites of great archaeological importance and interest.

In the Heart of Ireland, there we have Slane Castle, the Hill of Slane, the Hill of Tara which was the seat of the High Kings of Ireland. We have the town of Kells, Loughcrew, Dowth, 35 other structures as well as the Heart and Soul, of the 7 Celtic Nations, Newgrange.

And as of Saturday 14/July/2018 after a heatwave in Ireland, it was uploaded on the news, on Friday, a historian was flying a drone over the area and could visibly see that there are more structures buried underground, which gives us the opportunity to uncover further secrets held in our landscape. This is amazing, as our true heritage, our culture, all that has been buried on us by the Brit's monarchy, co-inside with the Roman Empire, could all very well be discovered. The Celtic Cross itself is 5000 years old, 3000 years older than Jesus's (Yeshua's) crucifixion where many religions were set up about. The real power, the true meaning, all stems from our Country, in Co. Meath, Ireland.

Now, to understand what occurred, New Grange's mound contained a secret that remained hidden for hundreds of years. The Romans visited New Grange in the years around 400, and their 'votive offerings' of coins and jewellery were recovered from the top of the mound during excavations. Coins were also found, still in mint condition within New Grange's tomb itself. They (the Romans) were also witnesses to the Sun appearing to walk on water and Rise on the 3rd day from the perspective of New Grange's, Sacred Irish site.

Gold coins scattered around the top of the mound indicates, the Irish keepers of this sacred site, we're not accepting currency from the Romans, for control of this monument, built for a loving awakening, to be used and most likely abused and under a controlling foreign power. So the deal went sower.

Two large skeleton bodies were found in New Grange site, which over time with encouraging false stories and cover ups, lead people to believe that our sites were burial tombs when discovered. But most likely, our ancestors did not want to be locked in or burnt alive in our most sacred site, the heart and soul of our 7 Celtic Nations!

The Hill of Tara in the Boyne Valley, a site associated with Kingship rituals, from the time of the first Celtic influence until the Roman invasion in the 12th Century, the Hill of Tara was Ireland's political and Spiritual capital. The King of Tara represented an ancient ideal of sacred Kingship in Ireland. Many Kings of Tara were also High Kings of Ireland.

I realise that there is not much-written information from our Celts, as due to the burning of our history by those who invaded Ireland. But studies show that Irish builders built Celtic Stonehenge along with tombs in England, Ireland, Scotland, Wales, and Brittany.

Knowth and Dowth in the Boyne Valley are several centuries older than Stonehenge. The studies show New Grange, and Stonehenge we're the centre of the action in Neolithic times.

The same designs and circles are on them. New Grange hints that the Celts may have not just started Western civilisation, but also saved it over the millennia's. And it's a proven fact that New Grange was built by knowledgeable and civilised people.

Many stories come out of Ireland, stories of Underworlds, the Salmon of Knowledge, Shamanism, and many great stories of inner wisdom and Self-Realisation that today's world is only starting to wake up to.

What's the real meaning of the story, The Leprechaun, The Rainbow and The Pot of Gold, that made its way around the world?

This is a story that the elders told the children so that the children could understand how to find real Gold. Gold is the most valuable material asset in the world. It's symbolic as it represents a state of awareness, which comes from within, this level of consciousness, is called Self-Realisation. The only way to explain Self-Realisation to a child is to define its materialistic definition called Gold.

Let's start off with the Leprechaun. The name came from Lugh, he was the Celtic warrior King Lugh. He was the father of the hero Cuchulainn, and when driven underground, he became little stooping Lugh which became anglicised to a leprechaun. Over the years, the dominant image diminished in favourite folk memory until he became merely a fairy craftsman named Lugh-Chromain "Little stooping Lugh," which became anglicised as Leprechaun. But this patron of arts and crafts name is remembered in the following places of many lands, not just Ireland: Lyons, Leon, Loudan and Laon in France, Lugo in Spain, Leiden in Holland as well as the capital city of England itself which, like Lyons, was named the "fortress of Lugh - Lugdunum, hence the Latin Londinium and then London.

But as the story goes, the Leprechaun is the Irish person, going to the end of the Rainbow to find their Pot of Gold. The Rainbow is made up of the seven different colours, that are within us and they are called Celtic Knots. The Celtic knot is a multi-dimensional and dynamic exploration of the body's energy system, illuminating a sacred pathway to evolve human consciousness.

These knots that are in every human being on the planet are called the Root, Sacral, Navel, Heart, Throat, Third Eye and Crown Knots. There are Seven knots, and each knot has a different colour, starting with Red, Orange, Yellow, Green, Blue, Indigo and Violet.

'Coincidently' enough, each Rainbow that you ever see is made up of precisely the same colours.

The bigger picture here is - As above – so below, as within – so without. Our outer world is a reflection of our inner world.

The Rainbow becomes in our vision because the Sun and the rain occur at the same time, this occurrence is consistently happening in Ireland as the Sun is there, but it always seems to rain. Rainbows appear in seven colours because the water droplets break white Sunlight into the seven colours of the spectrum, those exact colour's are mentioned above. You can only see a Rainbow if the Sun is behind you and the rain in front. The colours of the Rainbow are also within you and most importantly, the pathway to the Pot of Gold. (Elán)

The Gold over the Rainbow is Self-Realisation, it's consciousness, awakened. On the path to Elán, you expand yourself from receiving data from your present understanding to data that comes from outside your current timeline, it comes as a form of 'knowing' within, trust this knowledge.

Elàn is a Celtic Spirituality for Irish people; this is our birthright, knowledge, wisdom, understanding, compassion, and purity, all of the unconditionally loving, feel-good stuff, that's who we are! All on the path to awakening, to elevation and possible transcendence! To bring what man has tried to interpret as Heaven - to Earth.

The truth is, the Rainbow and the Pot of Gold (ELÁN) is there for everybody to reach a level of Self-Realisation.

Brigid, also known as Bride or Bridey, was a Celtic Healer; she was the traditional patroness of healing. She was a true teacher and scientist and healer. She taught that there was no separation between the inner and outer worlds. She was a true Irish Goddess in real Irish history. She was added to the new religion as St Bridget. Our history was robbed and integrated into a religion where some of it, you would agree with and some of it you may not.

The part you agree of, you'll find has come from our ancestors as deep within we are all connected on that level. The part where Jesus's (real name Yeshua) mother gave birth to a man without conceiving and that

Jesus had no girlfriend – Mary Magdalene and Rose on the 3rd day - is clearly not real.

This has, in turn, made sex bad without marriage (programmed by the church) and you should feel ashamed. Also implying men are superior to woman and many other false beliefs. It's a design to not only breed guilt, but to create as many offspring as possible (no contraceptive allowed) so that the power gets bigger over generations.

And Jesus was white? He was from Nazareth, Jerusalem – how many white people do you know from there?

This, in turn, has made white people superior and that was the plan.

Yeshua was the King of Hearts, but over the centuries, the organisations set up around him became the relative opposite of what it was supposed to be. The Romans empire finally collapsed in the 5th century and Roman Catholicism desperately needed to get back in control, they saw the Irish setting up Monasteries that, so effectively changed the barbaric ways of Europe to educated, civilised people, so gave it a temporary stamp of approval.

The Roman Empire saw a way, took over with religion about a man called Yeshua, who they called Jesus, who died on a cross - had a heart of gold (knowing the Irish have great empathy and we have the Celtic Cross in our history for 3200 years before this). The Irish held onto their education for as long as possible - but continuous attacks of control from all angles including two superpowers, who joined together finally changed that, but we didn't loose our power, it was just tested and we came through.

If you believe in a god or a higher power, know this, it's within you. You're not just a drop in the ocean; you are also the ocean in a drop. You are not only part of, but also, all of the Universe experiencing itself.

If you asked me – what did religion do to Ireland? I'd say, broke the Celtic people over generations with impositions of control and guilt.

I see how it's so effective because of what Ireland's goes through – so Ireland needs hope, religion is there, it's not the hope you need, but it's the only thing on offer. So you go for it because you're psychical, mentally and emotionally oppressed but the faith you go for – spiritually breaks you.

The question is, where does one find the answers? The answers are not outside of you but inside of you. It's all there once the four aspects of the Self-are in synchronisation – waiting for you to connect yourself to the Self, we're all connected on that level.

Religion teaches you separation, and if you're in one church, you can't go to another. The only one thing with many religions is – it's control, guilt and self-defeating. It's the 21st Century, and it's time to wake up.

It's objective is meant to get the people to be enlightened, and it certainly does not do that, and the empowered have their pockets full of so much money, in quite a lot of cases, by supporting them, you're just making the dangerous powers more powerful.

When the truth comes your way, your mind is not in conflict with it, as the same truth, is deep within each person, so it's a vibrational match. Although the truth might shake you around a little, it can't hurt you. The truth doesn't hurt people. It sets them free!

Let's get back to what's real?

New Grange has the 3 Swirles inside carved into the rock. The Shamrock is a fair representation of that. New Grange is real, but that's not its real name.

St Patrick is real – he did a lot of good stuff – which was drastically changed and did not work out in the end as the church of Rome took over but was probably goodish at that time as it slowed down the slave trade and kept people with their families.

All religion comes down to this. Treat others how you wish to be treated. What you give out - you get back. After educating myself by taking on this project. I have just changed the religion I was born into – to Agnosticism. Now I'm free. Agnosticism means I do not believe in any religion but if God came down and proved himself/herself to be God - I'd accept that. Gets me off the hook with all the controlling organisations out there and back to what's essential, to be free.

They took our knowledge of Spirituality, gave us a false religion, and tricked us into believing our own knowledge was evil.

It's just that lingering knowing within – the same Elàn knowledge that they don't have the depth themselves to understand. Yes, it's an Irish thing and a Celt thing, that inner knowing knows, we have been lied to – not to mention 5 genocides and a total fabrication of history, but it's the lingering knowing within, that's what's eating us alive.

All darkness must come to light.

As Damien Dempsey sings in his song, 'With the Roman Empire – the Shame came along. They called this Love - Evil, and they have done much harm'.

Let me just say, from being a proud Irish man living in Australia for the majority of the last 16 years, before we get into this, there are 5000-year-old pyramid artefacts found in Hunter Valley Caves near Sydney, Australia. Dutch DNA found in many Aussie people today – shipwrecked history says. But England discovering the world is false – they were just good at stealing cultures, writing history books and leaving populations so damaged, where the people had no choice but to read English history books and end up internalising their slant on history, in the hope to know something – but it's just not true.

Tasmania was named after Able Tasman after his 1642 discovery, who was Dutch, and sailed from Amsterdam. Then he discovered New Zealand. Able named Tasmania, Van Diemen's Land. There is a good movie called 'Van Diemen's' Land about a story of Eight Fenian men taken from Ireland by the Brits, who break out of a remote penal colony in Australia and find themselves faced with horrifying decisions in a battle for survival.

Things have got messy over the centuries; so let me give you the data that you're missing to see the bigger picture.

CHAPTER 2

Where it all Started

Well, the first Legend found in Èire (Ireland) was in 10,500BC and this is where our story begins.

There was a glacial period, and up until about 9000 years ago, a lot of Ireland was covered in ice, most of the time. At that stage in history, Ireland along with Britain was part of Europe. But during the ice age, rising sea levels due to ice melting caused Ireland to become separated from Britain and eventually Britain from Europe over the next 5000 years.

There is evidence in Ballycastle in the county of Mayo of an extensive field system, known as the Ceide fields, arguably the oldest in the world (in our recorded history) dating from 3500BC to 3000BC. One thousand hectares of land which is the worlds largest Neolithic site of cultural farmland.

Around 2500 BC, the Bronze Age began, which brought technology such as weaving textiles, the wheel, skilled metalworking which produced new weapons and tools along with brewing alcohol!

DNA is proven, with scientific strands of evidence that shows infinite details about a person, a race of people and countless information that apparently goes back to the 'big bang' if its understood correctly, which is always unfolding in new discoveries. Did you know the DNA found in the people of our 7 Celtic nations is different to many English decent people today? Here is why.

The Celts were a mighty race of people. Romans have recorded that the Celts are savages, barbaric and uncivilised. A point they made, demonstrated their view of this, when they went as far as to say, the Celts drank wine, which is not watered down unlike how the Romans drank wine. Seriously – the Celts drank wine straight, necked it, and that was their definition of savages!

When groups of people say these things – as all colonisers tend to do — it's usually a reflection of their own behaviour, in mirror image of themselves.

The Romans who believed in a crucifixion, gladiators fighting to the death and throwing people to the lions for entertainment, felt this was uncivilised – when you look at some of the histories out there, you got to realise two things, who wrote it and why? I would agree that the Celts in Ireland would manage a straight bottle of wine, but with the rest of what they said, was just made up lies to get support, to justify their actions – the plan was always to expand and take over and attempt to control the population.

Let's look at our history; St Patrick is a fascinating subject. Born 385 in Wales – died 17/March/461.

Irish King, Niall of the Nine Hostages, took a hostage from each trading place, which is called England today but was broken up into provinces with seperate Kings in the 5th century. Niall took a hostage from Merica, Northumbriea, East Anglia, Essex, Kent, Sussex, Jutes, Hastings and even France, in order to get them all to trade fairly. Patrick was a boy from Wales and one of the hostages, who's father was a Roman Briton priest. Patrick grew up in Ireland working on the land and looking after animals, where he got visions of a religious nature. After 7 years he left Ireland and at some stage later went for a job interview with the Roman church.

Romans had their eye on Ireland for adding to the Roman Christianity. Patrick went for the job interview in Rome. Succat was his name, replaced by Patricius in Rome and ended up being called Patrick by the Irish. Patrick believed Christianity was the true religion and Irish beliefs to change, taking hostages for one example for fair trading.

There were 5 main Kings in Ireland, one for each area, Ulster, Munster, Leinster and Connacht, and Meath! With 100-150 other Kings beneath them. Patrick came back to Ireland in later years, trying to convert the people. Patrick has to convince the Irish that Christianity was the way to salvation. Irish people scattered all over Ireland - but he started his work in a barn.

He realised that he needed to convert the Kings to make true lasting progress. The Shamrock was introduced as, the Father, Son and Holy Ghost. Patrick's authority came from the Pope to banish the snakes from Ireland, snakes were said to be peoples sins.

Patrick lite a fire on the Hill of Tara and was brought in front of the King. He entertained the King with his ideas and was allowed convert the people, if they choose to be converted.

This was the High King called Laoghaire, after whom Dun Laoghaire is named and he was killed, in the Slide of Saggart – he was a son of the previous King called Niall of the 9 Hostages. The King didn't punish Patrick for his disrespectful act, as he knew Patrick as the boy Succat, the boy who was taken as hostage by his father.

Everything soon changed, Irish monks were talking Latin and teaching Greek philosophy, and educational books were at hand. Many things changed, and the Legend of Croagh Patrick symbolises the power of that Revolution.

The Celts had a highly sophisticated Spiritual system, with three types of Druids; the Bards – who knew the songs and stories of the tribe, the Ovates – who were the healers and seers and the Druids – who were the philosophers, judges, and teachers. St Patrick's Monks of his time recorded all the old Druid laws of Ireland, which we still have a record of in Ireland.

A man called Patrick managed to change everything, and we celebrate St Patrick every year, it's a great day. But what are we celebrating I decided to research. How did Patrick persuade a people profoundly into their Celtic ways to be part of Christianity?

Well, we the Celts celebrated the end of the month of December as the days got darker and from our perspective, the sun appeared to walk on water, being perceived as still for 2 days, and moved into re-birth, as on the 3rd day it rose and we celebrated with fires and music and the craic each year at the Hill of Tara to finish off the old and welcome a new year.

Patrick kept the Celtic beliefs but changed the Sun in the sky to Christ the Son of God. The Celtic Druids were members of the educated, professional class among the Celtic people of Ireland who, an expert in their field, informed the population of their discoveries, our history, and our ways. The sacred water of the druids became the holy water of baptism. The number three held great significance in the Celtic tradition. We have the mind, body, spirit and also inside New Grange, the foundation is engraved on the rock inside, consisting of three Spirals connected. Patrick applied this Celtic understanding; everything works in three's knowledge ingeniously by using a shamrock that grew in Ireland to explain the Christian concept, of a triune God, the father, the son and the holy spirit that are each a separate element of just one entity.

The druids got hostile towards Patrick; they saw Patrick as a deadly enemy as he was preaching a different message and weaning people from the Celtic Spirituality to this new religion.

Patrick made the transfer from the things the druids passionately believed in and in order for Patrick to fulfil his visions, Patrick replaced a way of life with another way of life which people found much more satisfactory at that time. We are looking at 1500 years ago. Patrick was totally against slavery – and the people liked his ideas, no more slavery. Patrick could read and write, and he brought Latin to Ireland. It wasn't just a new religion but a Social and Political Revolution.

What about alcohol? It was nice to hear St Patrick brought liquor to Ireland – stuff you will find on the Internet but alcohol was invented 2,500BC before recorded time started – by the Celts and to be honest, I wouldn't say we were the first on the planet to have a drink – you know – recently they are looking into civilisations dating back 100,000's of years now.

But stories say Patrick fasted on a hilltop for 40 days and 40 nights and stories that he drove the snakes out of Ireland. Science shows us that there were never any snakes in Ireland.

Snake has a few meanings, for example, when a person is related to as a Snake, the meaning is a very dishonest, untrustworthy, person.

And when a healer heals a person from emotional baggage, heavy dense energy, he refers to it as, 'it was like pulling a snake out of the person'.

Also, contradictory to that, snakes all over the world are respected, they shed their skin, re-birth and also the symbol for world medicine is a snake.

Patrick establishes churches across the country - and 350 bishops. He managed to establish Christianity in Ireland and died 17 March - which became a session day! Worldwide!

So, the story goes, St Patrick drove the snakes out of Éire and sowed the seeds of a new civilisation.

Britain

Now, across the water, England at this same time in history – things were different. It was a Roman province called Britannia. Boats of heavily armed men rowed to Britannia.

They were Saxons, Jutes, Angles, and Frisians. Like the Irish, these tribes were never subjugated by the Roman Empire. It seems as though they were mercenaries who were invited in by the Romans, to fight against tribes like the Picts (Scottish) and the Irish. But it did not go according to plan. Sure many were Celtic tribes themselves.

The Romans messed up. They, being mercenaries, slaughtered a lot of the Roman soldiers and took over the country, what we call England today but were a Roman province then.

The Romans didn't give up, but they lost the battles against the Welsh (also Celts) and what we call Scotland today; they too belonged to a tribe called the Picts (also Celts) who kept most of the land we call Scotland today. The Scots moved to the Highlands to regroup. A Roman army went into Scotland to take over, and they were never seen or heard of again – vanished! A wall was later built by the Romans to protect themselves from the Picts. But the mercenaries took over Britannia.

The places were called East Saxons, West Saxons, Eastern Angles, Mercian's and over time the name became England, and their new language became English.

The Welsh were never conquered, and the Welsh language is the actual native language for the Britannia people.

So basically England was taken over by Saxons and Ireland was embracing a new religion.

A lot was going on, monasteries were set up over Ireland, monks were high on education, speaking Gaelic but teaching Greek and Latin and it wasn't just religion – there were better technologies, better ways of building and libraries and modern hospitals were set up. Also, there's something we need to realise here; the Irish Monks were allowed to marry and have children, they had families!

St Patrick's father is believed to have been a priest and even Patrick had a wife and children. The early Irish Christian church was Greek rite and allowed as it does today for their clergy to marry.

Leinster man Columbán taught a Celtic Monastic Rule. Born in 543 and passed away on 21/November/615. He set up Monasteries from around 590 in places like the Frankish and Lombard Kingdoms; he set up Luxeuil Abbey in France and Bobbio Abbey in Italy and StGallen in Switzerland.

Columbán is one of the earliest identifiable Hiberno-Latin writers. He did all this work to educate and civilise the people of Europe who had been overrun by barbarians. He set up five monasteries in total and passed away at Bobbio.

The Irish are the only ones who have a blueprint of the architectural drawings of a highly crafted designed monastery, and they built masterpieces.

In the middle of the 5th century, the Roman Empire collapsed, and the Saxons drove the Roman influence, out of Britannia. Romans are considered to have built Sub-Roman divisions in England then.

But here we are in the middle of the 6th century, and the new craze is religion. Mind you, the new religion of Ireland is Celtic Christianity, Irish owned, not controlled by Rome. Irish held, Irish Monasteries.

So Britain was still pagan and very much barbaric, and the rest of Europe became civilised and educated due to Irish man Columbán and his crew. A lot was going on, and it was good for that time. Britain was an illiterate and a backward place, so the Celts decided to bring them intelligent information in order to help civilise the country.

It started around 565AD, when 12 Irish monks went to Scotland. Columba as now known, was born in 521, his name was Colm Cille who was an Irish abbot, who went to Scotland and converted Scotland to Celtic Christianity. He set up Church Dove in Iona, Scotland. He is the patron saint of Derry, he was highly regarded by the Geals and the Pics, and remembered today as one of the 12 apostles of Ireland and known throughout Ireland, Scotland, and all the western world.

It was the most important thing on the British Isles to be converted to Christianity as the church taught people how to rear their children, bury their dead and day to day living along with writing and building technologies. It changed everything – so when you look at it, the Celts saved Britain, they turned it from a wild, hostile place to an educated, civilised society.

After education and civilised power were brought in by the Celts, many of the priests in England started to look at the Roman religion and their rituals and different ways instead of Irish ways as these religions were the craze back then, it was changing barbaric ways to civilised ways for a while.

Around 665AD, Easter came and conflict arose. You see, the King of England learned his teachings from Irish Monks. But his wife grew up in Kent and was under the Roman Christianity that was flourishing, so they disagreed with the timing of Easter.

There was a time difference between setting the time of lent in the Celtic church and that of the Roman religion. I'm not joking, but the King wanted private time with his wife in the bedroom, but she was still on lent, as she was to be on-lent for another week and religion forbid anyone to have an action time on lent.

Shit hit the fan but not just this; there was a conflict between two Christian factions. Ireland had their Church of Celtic humble origin and teachings but faced the Roman Church whose ways took over Europe and many parts of the world.

There's always a choice in life, but only two options and that was, either be part of the Irish Church or the Roman Church, which was Europe mainstream religion.

So the King of England had a choice to make. He went with the Roman religion because it was more important to him, in the sense that most of Europe, was under the Roman doctrine. It was like joining a currency – a currency of faith, a way of being part of Europe.

Columba had been the leading man in Scotland, and he was Celtic and part of Celtic Christianity. Ireland also brought power to England and not long afterward, England used that power against the Irish. So the Celtic church changed from Greek rite to Roman rite with all it entailed.

In the 700's Vikings descended on the monasteries of Ireland, rounded up many monks and slaughtered them and the great age of Irish Christianity was almost brought to an end.

CHAPTER 3

Perspective

Let's go back a notch, let's look at this from another perspective. When recorded time started, not just the clocks started, but the psychological time held in the minds of people was to be the greatest curse that faced our world for the last two millennia. As with time continuously ticking in the minds with endless thoughts, creates a psychological time, leading to the illusion of a better future, whilst a present hell is created to fulfil that.

There was Celtic wisdom there, so powerful, that although Ireland did so much good for Europe (changed it from barbaric to civilised, not to mention the masterpieces built), still the Roman Empire felt they needed control and power, and they needed to try get rid of what the Celts knew. Lets call it the Yin and the Yang forces at work.

We had our own Chiefs and our own Kings in Ireland, Niall Noígíallach was in power around 380. It was his bloodline that ruled Ireland for several centuries, his descendants were known as the Uí Néill. Niall was the 126th High King of Ireland and legend says, the greatest High King of Ireland. Irish rulers had responsibility to their people and were loved by their people.

He was involved in raids into Britain whilst it was Roman-ruled, Caesar (Roman leader) had a few failed attempts on taking over all the land but managed to take over England at that time. Romans were not successful against the Celts of Ireland, Scotland, Wales, Isle of man, Cornwall, Brittany, and Galicia.

Niall established a dynasty of powerful chieftains that dominated the island for six centuries. It was a great society, advanced society, just Celtic people, looking out for each other, abundance in food, living off the land, creating music, arts and dancing, a culture full of philosophers, teachers and communities, looking out for each other and rearing their children.

The Romans in history books will say Irish were barbaric and you'll see why they said those things. King Niall died in Roman Britain, defending Ireland.

We had Kings in Ireland for centuries. Brian Ua Néill was the last one who died in 1260 and no other Gaelic King was ever again recognised as King or High King of Ireland.

We had Queens, Queens were not uncommon in the Christian world. An Irish Queen would have been like the mother of all mothers caring for her people in the most loving way. Queen Maeve of Connaught for one example.

Due to the intellectual and Spiritual stimulation of the Irish monks, the Abbey at Luxeuil became the most important and flourishing monastery in what was called Gaul at that time.

The work and skills and deep education of numbers are all in his work and is still very interesting to this day to see the genius skills within the structures of the buildings. All his great efforts, building masterpieces and work he did, were stolen one way or another by the Roman Empire.

Everything about the Irish people has been stolen and re-written into history by the British Empire or Roman Empire, and many times by both empires at once.

Who discovered America? Columbus, an Italian explorer – taught by British history! I guess Columbán's name was so ingrained in Europe over the amazing work he did that history couldn't rub out the name. So the name continued on but in a different fashion. History tells Columbus as an explorer. Columbus's real name was Cristóbal Colón.

Also, who really discovered America from Europe – keep in mind the Native (Indian) American's have been there for thousands of years. But an Irish man called Brendan sailed to America in the 6th Century, a thousand years before Columbus, in a timber-framed boat, sealed with leather skins, stitched together, with a crew of about 20 men.

Brendan was known for establishing churches in Britain and Ireland and voyaging with other monks to various islands in the vicinity, all in a small currach, which is a traditional Irish boat with a wooden frame wrapped in leather.

All the achievements of Ireland's discoveries have been buried and the history re-written by the British Empire and the Roman Empire.

Sure wasn't it also true that electricity was discovered in Maynooth, Ireland, by the Irish Monks – but Brits came along, took it and levelled the area.

The Irish wanted to bring wisdom, free energy and education to Europe – just like their Celtic ancestors did. It's a gene in the Irish DNA to bring wisdom, love, peace, joy, education, philosophy and understanding and the craic to Europe and the world.

Vikings

In the 700's, we had Viking raids in Ireland. In 795 the first Viking raid appeared in Ireland, Rathlin Island off the coast of Antrim where the church was burned. On the west coast, Monasteries on Inismurray and Inishbofin were plundered by the raiders.

The Scottish Island of Iona was also attacked the same year. Many robberies took place, with many monks killed, hit and run attacks which happened from the coast. There's no evidence of attacks more than twenty miles inland.

The raids were difficult to defend but the Vikings were many times defeated. These raids went on for 41 years. The Vikings had raided around the coast and the Island Monastery of Sceilg, off Kerry Coast. The Monastic city of Armagh was attacked three times in 832.

The Vikings only wanted to raid and plunger, the monks had the gold and the fine hand made jewelries, the attacks were yearly, unpredictable and hard to stop due to the isolation of the areas, which were all beside the ocean, until we have Ivar the boneless who sought conquest. Dublin town was set up by the Vikings as a trading place - it's first buildings was built by Ivar the boneless and Olaf the White - A Danish King in the 840's. It became a trading place with places across Europe and it got cashed up and it became a successful city.

Irish took on the Vikings and many battles took place. Over time, they mixed in and married and had Irish-Viking kids. Ivar and Olaf went across the ocean and took most of Britain from Kingdom to Kingdom in 870, and both returned to Dublin in triumph. Ivar by then was known as King of all the Norsemen of all Ireland and Britain and he later passed away in 873.

Those settled Vikings became Irish over time, but more Vikings then came and more battles occurred. But the overall picture of what the

Vikings did was set up many towns beside the ocean for transport and trading. And also the Irish learned from these experiences, that they need to be united, a national structure put in place, to defend Ireland from Vikings or other raiders.

From that, Brian Baru became High King of Ireland - succeed his brother in Munster and although he was born to be a military leader, still had a kind heart and was loved by the people.

After the Celtic Christianity education was burnt and monks slaughtered – over time, the Vikings settled in Ireland, mixed in with society and soon enough over a short few generations became Irish. There is very little to zero DNA from the Vikings found in Ireland today.

After the Vikings

The Celts were untouchables – it's important to realise that what was to later happen to Ireland under British rule was caused by the Crown, the British controlling Empire and not the English people that you meet today that just happened to be born in the country, (as the Aussie's refer - POMS - Prisoners Of Majesties Service.)

In order to take over a race of people, they needed to break the people physically, mentally, emotionally and spiritually.

Roman Empire failed to control on a psychical, emotional and mental level, so they took control spiritually.

Narcissistic wounded people never give up; they just turn into aggressors with the same agenda, control. Aggressors like psychopaths are fully aware of what they are doing; they just don't have the human capacity to feel empathy. In this day and age, we have an abundance of narcissists and psychopaths and many Irish people with a lot of Empathy.

In 1155, Pope Adrian IV, a British born Pope of the Roman Catholic Church, issued a papal bull known as a Laudabiliter. This gave King Henry II of England permission to invade Ireland as a means of taking control over the Irish Church.

This invasion was planned by the King of England, and the Pope of the Roman Catholic Church, – both with their own agendas but uniting for the same control and power cause.

The Norman invasion of Ireland began in 1169, under the authority of this bull. Pope Alexander III, ratified the Laudabiliter and gave King Henry (according to Pope Alexander), dominion over the 'barbarous nation' of Ireland so that its 'filthy practices' may be abolished, its church finally brought into line after 300 years and accept the Roman rite and that the Irish pay their tax to Rome.

After the Norman mercenary invasion of Ireland, 36 more Acts and Treaty's were set up over the next 800 years involving Ireland, Wales, and Scotland.

The Pope (first and last British pope in Rome) wanted control of Irish Churches. King Henry wanted Ireland. The Pope passed the bill. It was already. Then Dairmait Mac Murchada, King of Leinster, looked for help off the British King to regain control over his Kingdom after domestic differences. This military intervention had the backing of King Henry and Pope Adrian IV. The Leinster King really messed up but the Storm was coming one way or another, they were just waiting for away in.

More Norman mercenary landings arrived in Ireland, led by Richard Strongbow de Clare. They took Leinster, Dublin, Waterford, and Wexford.

The High King of Ireland led counterattacks against the Normans but didn't get a lot of the conquered territory back.

In 1171, King Henry brought in a large Anglo-Norman army into Ireland to take control of both the Normans and the Irish.

The Norman lords gave their conquered territory to Henry. Henry let Strongbow hold Leinster and he declared the cities to be Crown land.

The Kings of Ireland submitted to Henry in the hope that the Norman expansion would come to an end. Henry, however, granted the unconquered Kingdom of Meath to Hugh de Lacy. When Henry left in 1172, Norman expansion and Irish counteroffensives continued.

In 1175 false documents were set up. This made Henry overlord of the conquered territory and Ruaidrí O Conner, as overlord of the rest of Ireland once he swears to King Henry.

That idea fell apart as the Anglo-Norman lords invaded Irish Kingdoms and they, in turn, launched counterattacks.

So in 1177, King Henry declared his son John to be 'Lord of Ireland' and he ordered the Normans to invade more land.

Normans are raiders and pirates from Denmark, Iceland, and Norway who under their leader Rollo gave their name to Normandy, a region in France.

This was a clever take over by King Henry, using the Norman mercenaries and the backing of the Roman Catholic Church. They all wanted Ireland.

It was a successful invasion over many years because the Normans were military mercenaries, (more and more were sent into Ireland until the Irish finally break), the King of Leinster was having some conflict with the other Kings which made them temporarily weak and Henry had the Roman Church's support for Henry's intervention. Clever but pure evil. This was the start of the 750 years of Hell on Earth.

It was impossible for the Irish to win in this situation, there was only to be a breaking point.

CHAPTER 4

Roman Religion

L et's just call a spade a spade - Roman Religion was the greatest curse to hit Ireland. Not only because of Crusades, killings in the name of a God, molesting's, deposing of children because of unwed parents but it never brought enlightenment to people, only hell itself.

You see – The Roman Empire and the Celtic people had a problem, Roman Empire wanted to conquer, Celts wished to live at one with nature and harmony, to educate people and to have a society lifted up to love, peace, joy, compassion, truth, and kindness – to an awakening.

This is why the Irish Celts built all these places like New Grange – Stonehenge, and the masterpieces throughout Europe, to move the people to the next level!

Battles took place because the Roman Empire wanted to take over; Celts, strong and powerful, full of mystery and wisdom defended themselves for millennia's. It is controlling narcissistic psychopaths V's the powerful Celtic Empathy culture. The religion forced upon us was an operation designed to control the people, disguised as hope, but feeding guilt. It was the only way to mess up Irish people's beliefs, and it did. The worst thing in history is by far the strict rules of the Roman Catholic Church.

There are some truths in religion, there are some truths in every religion, and there's a lot of stuff that is not true – man wrote these books and written at a time that it could benefit the current situation at that time, whatever the writer's agenda was, which was occult control.

Symbols, experiences, and stories from the Celtic knowledge were used in this religion, which made it compelling and this was the operation used to control many people over generations. Not only that, let's get to the effectiveness of this operation.

Christianity was developed in an Era of the Roman Empire, the same time many religions were in practice. There was Greco-Roman religions, the Roman imperial cult, philosophic monotheistic religions called Neo-Platonism and Gnosticism and also the Tribal Spiritualities from the Celts, Picts, Saxons, Jutes, Angles and Frisians who were never conquered by the Romans. The rituals of Celtic Spirituality, Germanic paganism, Slavic paganism, and folk religion influenced Christianity.

The Roman Empire took the profound truths and wisdom within each religion and Pagan Spirituality and from that combined wisdom, made their story to control the population.

This was why it was so effective. The Roman Catholic Church has a long history of deception and corruption. Aside from committing acts of genocide, it is undoubtedly one of the most corrupt organisations in history – that unfortunately still goes on today in this awakening of the 21st Century!

Knowledge – Wisdom – Awakening to the truth within you, gives people power, self-awareness and infinite wisdom of the Self and the Universe. Basically the more you know about you - the less there is to know - full stop! The real aim of awakening is to get to a level of awareness called Self-Realisation.

Many religions keep people in their minds, questioning everything and restricts the person from awakening with false beliefs. It imprisons the person in a state of mind – rather than allowing the person to be conscious, aware and free within a state of being. Religion renders people powerless. Awakening to the truth gives people back their power.

In Latin, religion means prison. 'None are more hopelessly enslaved than those who falsely believe they are free!'

"The christian religion is a parody on the worship of the sun, in which they put a man called christ in the place of the sun, and pay him the adoration originally payed to the sun". Thomas Paine 1737-1809.

In Christian religion, the Old Testament is Joseph and New Testament is Jesus but the whole story is plagiarised from the Egyptian Religion and Moses's 10 commandments is all taken from the Egyptian book of the dead.

The Roman Empire sent many people into Ireland over a millennium to bring Roman religion to Ireland. The British Empire (descendants of the Roman Empire) came in and burnt all our books, recorded wisdom from our ancestors the Irish Celts, buried New Grange site, changed the names of every significant bit of culture we had and many attempts were made to take our power away, over this operation that would not give up on control.

A few hundred years later, in England, King Henry had a dispute with Rome. It was first called defender of the faith for treatises he wrote on Catholicism. His marriage failed to produce a son and heir, so Henry wanted to divorce, to remarry, and this brought him into conflict with the Roman religion, ultimately ending with Henry proclaiming himself head of the Church of England and Ireland. He wanted to set up his own faith or at least change it, as religion was basically law back in those days, and it was a very effective way of controlling the population.

You see; if you change a person's beliefs, their mentality is changed, their actions are changed, their words are changed, and their behaviour is also changed.

What people talk about is what's on their minds, what's on their minds, comes from what they believe. What you believe is all you see in your world, which reinforces your belief and your outside is a reflection of your inside, so what you consider to be true becomes true for you. The church teaches you and gets you to believe its version of the truth - a fake story. Once you believe it, your mind filters out anything that gets in the way of those beliefs. For example, Da Vinci's painting of the Last Supper has been out since the 1500's, the artist is sending a message, and no one can see that Jesus has a girlfriend right next to him in the painting, as they have been programmed to believe that it's twelve male apostles. A belief even stops the eyes from working. Beliefs are powerful, so we should be careful what we believe, (at least question our possible beliefs before setting them as beliefs.)

Then there is Roman Julius Cesar at the foundation of this religion in 100AD. He used to have sex with his generals, in a way to demonstrate ownership and to subjugate them so they will never take over from him, as they become shamed broken people. This ownership and control tactic filtered throughout the organisation from generation to generation until what we have today in Ireland and many other countries under this roman catholic religion.

And another thing to wrap our heads around is - people don't see things as they are, they see things as how THEY are, which causes many miss-interpretations regarding interpreting any religious stories.

I would like to explain what I believe to be true for each individual, based on a lifetime of experiences, of this whole scale, of the Alpha to the Omega. I see that my outside world becomes a reflection of my inside world if the inside is not addressed and by understanding this, not only can one choose to end their pain and suffering, but by awareness can also choose to get to any level of consciousness.

We as people can range between the emotions and awareness in the whole spectrum between the Alpha and the Omega. We have about 17 levels of consciousness, degrees of emotions, levels of understanding on the path to ultimate Self-Realisation.

They range from, starting at Ultimate Consciousness to many degrees of Suffering.

Enlightenment
Peace
Joy
Love
Reason
Acceptance
Willingness
Neutrality
Courage
Pride
Anger
Desire
Fear
Grief
Apathy
Guilt
Shame.

Religions keep us on levels from Desire down to Shame. Understanding our true culture, looking within for truth, and our Slane heritage can take us up the levels to Enlightenment.

You see, many religions do the opposite of what they're supposed to be doing, and in programming our minds, set up beliefs that restrict us.

We need to try to see the bigger picture and let those beliefs that don't serve us anymore be released or changed one at a time.

Just thought I would let you know, we are a client state of England and are under the control of the Roman Catholic Church, perhaps the two most controlling powers in the world and its time to wake up and set ourselves free from this delusional slavery.

David Bowie said, 'Religion is for people who fear hell, spirituality is for people who have been there'.

CHAPTER 5

Genocides

The real history of Ireland and the Irish people consists of many acts of genocide. It's absolutely incredible how the Celtic spirit still lives after what we as a race of people have been through, throughout the millennia.

All darkness must come to light for healing purposes. The story needs to be told otherwise, unfortunately, history repeats itself until changed. Knowledge and awareness of the actual history, allows us to move into the awakening of the 21st Century, through understanding and acceptance, healing and moving forward, holding within the proudness of both our Irish Resilience and our Irish Endurance.

One of the greatest lies taught in Ireland by Brit history books is the famine which was in fact genocide. Irish at the time called it, 'An Gorta Mór' meaning The Great Hunger which was a period of mass starvation, disease and organised genocide, in Ireland between 1845 and 1849.

The reason many of us Irish people didn't know our real history is because the truth has been covered up by the people who did the psychopathic acts. They covered up the truth about what really took place by propaganda and by writing their grandiose version in their history books. But the Irish Celtic people left trails of evidence everywhere in Ireland.

Let's start with the First Genocide. The British Empire stole Irish land, that's what they did with much of the area on the planet. The King of Britain then changed his religion to Protestant. Then made it a law in Ireland, if Irish Catholics don't become Protestants, they are moved off their land.

Basically, Irish people had no rights to our land, in our own country. The British Empire stole 89% of the land. Oliver Cromwell who was a dictator in England moved the Irish from the fertile soils to the west of Ireland. Mass murder took place, and then he put many Irish on slave ships and sold them to the West Indies and colonial America.

The Irish were sold as slaves and worked as slaves in the West Indies and America. While the Irish were slaves, many Irish and African Americans intermingled and this is why you have many black people with Irish names today and Irish accents in the West Indies.

The Brits stole the land, held the crops, had the Irish work at farming, fed the Irish potatoes and made Irish people pay a tax, to live in a rented shack, on their own land, that they built themselves.

Those who attained a tiny portion of land, throughout the generations, the family would leave the small piece of land to their eldest son, while the rest of the children must emigrate to survive. The Catholic religion was outlawed – so the persecutions occurred.

You see, the Irish owned Ireland, but around this time before the famine, the colonising Brits held 89% of Irish land as they stole it. Colonisers take land, this is what they did, they stole land from the Native Americans in America, the Aboriginals in Australia, stole land in India, Canada, and South America, New Zealand and they stole it from the Irish in Ireland. It was a business model of Empire.

The Second Genocide was the Tudor conquest of Ireland in the 16th century. During 1536-1691, the first full conquest by England took place, and it involved colonisation by Britain by Protestant settlers. It was about transforming the Irish Gaelic structure to monarchical state governed society. It was run by King Henry the 8th, many battles took place and when the Irish Catholic Jacobites finally surrendered at Limerick, this confirmed British protestant dominance in Ireland.

King Henry VIII broke with Papal authority in 1536. He broke English Catholicism from Rome. His son Edward later broke with Papal doctrine completely. So many English became Protestant, some of the Protestants moved into Wales and became Welsh, some of the Protestants moved into Scotland and became Scottish while the Irish remained mainly Catholic. A full attempt to take over from all angles of the Celtic nations.

Queen Elizabeth broke with Rome later in 1570. For the next 400 years, Britain colonised Ireland. The terms of this power were that anyone who was not protestant was excluded.

Land rights is the solution in this 21st Century!

So in Ireland, we then had Welsh, Scottish and English landlords and to really confuse the situation, the English newspapers in history called them Irish landlords, as a means of saying, we didn't steal the land, sure, they're Irish landlords.

The Anglo-Normans were sent into Ireland by King Henry VIII when the King of Leinster asked for a little bit of help with a minor domestic situation. The Tudor conquest gave the Lambert's and many other clans land in Ireland. Ireland was stolen.

Then we have our long lost cousins, the Irish slaves. James II sold 30,000 Irish prisoners (those who tried to take their own food, that they grew themselves, to feed their own kids — were called convicts) as slaves to the West Indies to British settlers. And by the 1600s, Irish were the main slaves sold to Montserrat – a British overseas territory known as a Caribbean Island which at that time held 70% of the total population as Irish slaves and Antigua – a Leeward Island in the Caribbean region, which in the '80s found independence!

The Transatlantic Slave Trade consisted of Irish, men, women and children brought on British ships to what was called the New World – America. Those who rebelled on the boat, were poorly treated. Those who rebelled on land, slave owners hung their human property up and set their feet on fire. Some were burned alive, and some had their heads placed on pikes in the marketplace as a warning to other captives.

Oliver Cromwell was a big player in deporting Irish from Ireland and selling them as slaves. From 1641-1652 another 300,000 were sold as slaves. Families were separated, and the British Empire wouldn't allow the fathers to take their wives and children, and this lead to a helpless population of homeless women and children and Britain's solution was to auction them off as well.

In the 1650s, 100,000 Irish children between ten and fourteen years of age, removed from their parents, sold as slaves to the West Indies, Virginia and New England (a state in the States).

During this period, 52,000 women and children, sold to Barbados and Virginia. In 1656, Cromwell ordered his men to take 2000 Irish children from their parents and sold to the highest bidder in Jamaica to British settlers. Bob Marley's father was Irish and reared by British colonists, thus explains why so many Irish friends connect with Bob and his amazing freedom inspiring music.

African slaves kicked off around the same time, but they were ten times the price of Irish slaves.

It was never a crime to beat an Irish slave to death or a North American Indian. If an Irish woman somehow obtained her freedom, her kids would still remain slaves of their master, there was no getting out of slavery. The British Empire came up with an idea, and that was to breed Irish slaves, many girls as young as twelve years of age, with African slaves, to make more slaves, more workforces and more money.

These slaves were produced with a distinct complexion and were called 'mulatto' slaves who were more expensive than the Irish slaves. More money for the British establishment and less money paid out by the British settlers as opposed to African slaves.

This practice of breeding Irish women with African slave men went on for several decades – it became so widespread that in 1681 legislation was passed forbidding this practice. Not out of any sort of empathy, it was only stopped because it was interfering with the profits of a larger slave transport company and the colour issue, lighter colour people were being bred. Cassius Clay Mohammed Ali is the product of such a practice.

The Brits shipped out tens of thousands of slaves for more than a century. There was a 1798 Irish rebellion/uprising, and thousands of Irish slaves were sold to America and Australia. A man called John was a young army officer, who was an atheist but held Republican views. John was approached by the Sheares brothers - true Irishmen, who were Irish lawyers to join the United Irishmen – before the planned 1798 uprising. John secretly reported all the conversations had with the Sheares brothers – to his superior officers and the Sheares brothers got arrested. John was the most damaging witness at their trail. The Sheares brothers were tried on the 12 July 1798 and were hanged, drawn and quartered on the 14th. John made a speech in his defence and quoted "It is not the death which I am about to suffer that I deserve - no punishment could be adequate to such a crime." He showed some regret, but it was too late.

The slavery continued, Irish were taken to America and Australia. Elvis Presley's grandfather was a farmer in Co.Wicklow who was savagely beaten and hounded off his land. He left Ireland August 25th, 1775.

Ned Kelly is Australia's Icon, his father John "Red" Kelly was sentenced to Australia after stealing his own pig on his own land in Ireland at age 21 and incarcerated in Van Diemen's Land (Tasmania). Kelly is just one of an estimated half a million Irish people transported to Australia between 1788 and 1921, according to the National Museum of Australia. Ancestry.ie exposes this information.

The abuse was so severe, some didn't make the trip, and one British ship dumped 1,300 slaves into the Atlantic Ocean so that his crew would have plenty of food to eat. 1839, Britain stopped doing this transporting of slaves. But this didn't stop pirates from continuing, but the new law slowly ended the nightmare of Irish misery.

History books conveniently forgot to mention these facts, but none of the forgotten Irish heroes ever made it back to their homeland to describe their ordeal. But many Irish decent legends pop up around the world and help make the world a better place with music and creativity and fundamentally inspiring cultures worldwide. There is a book written about this called 'White Cargo' if you would like to explore more on our history of Irish slaves. Our long lost cousins are still out there somewhere and everywhere.

We discussed Cromwell shipping out Irish slaves, but this is how he did it. He was a religious fundamentalist and a general of his 'Model Army' to be the best fighting force in the whole of Europe, he had every man fighting in God's name. Once they got to Ireland, this crusading army marched in line, side by side from the north to the south massacring any Catholic in its path and by 1655, not a single Catholic landowner remained on the fertile land, east of the River Shannon. Then he shipped many of the remaining Irish off as slaves.

More about this on the net called Irish: The forgotten white slaves.

CHAPTER 6

An Grota Mór – 'Famine' - The Great Hunger.

The song called the 'Fields of Athenry' tells the story of this time in our Irish History.

'Michael they have taken you away, for you stole Trevelyn's corn, so the young might see the morn', as the lyrics go, 'now a prison ship awaits on the bay'.

Trevelyan family emigrated to America, Australia, and New Zealand with many Irish and Scottish stolen populations and the cycle continued. Trevelyan was also responsible for the Scottish Highland clearances and some families from St Kilda being transported to Australia where they live to this day.

During the height of the famine, it is suggested that 'Trevelyan deliberately dragged his feet in disbursing direct government food and monetary aid to the Irish due to his strident belief in laissez-faire economics and the free hand of the market'.

He wrote a letter and in it, he described the famine as an "effective mechanism for reducing surplus population" as well as "the judgment of God" and wrote, "The real evil with which we have to contend is not the physical evil of the Famine, but the moral evil of the selfish, perverse and turbulent character of the Irish people."

Trevelyan never expressed remorse for his comments, even after the full dreadful scope of the Irish famine became known.

It has been said, "Trevelyan's most enduring mark on history may be the quasi-genocidal anti-Irish racial sentiment he expressed during his term in the critical position of administrating relief for the millions of Irish peasants suffering under the Irish famine as Assistant Secretary to HM Treasury (1840-1859) under the Whig administration of Lord Russell."

Trevelyan stole many Irish people and many Scottish High landers and shipped them to Australia. When he was questioned about this, he replied, "The Irish and Scotch, especially the latter, do much better when they have a fresh start in other countries and become mixed up with other people, than they stay at home."

The British Empire owned (stole) the crops – they weren't about to part with money for trade or food, they sent it all out and starved the Irish in their own country.

You see Irish were forced to eat potatoes as the only food readily available to them, as the British Empire landowners commandeered all the barley, eggs, butter, bacon and wheat and cattle plus the rest. Ireland was the breadbasket for England. But even if we forget our country was stolen, Ireland was a Colony of England at this time and therefore the people of Ireland were under the responsibility of the British Empire and duty of care was non-existent yet again – disease, starvation, and pestilence – order of the day.

The British Empire made a decision to remove all the food out of Ireland and deliberately starve the Irish population.

So this is in fact another Genocide. Starvation, deportation, and killings are ways to wipe out a population.

An Gorta Mór – The Great Hunger.
Census in Ireland
Year 1821 – People 6,801,827.
Year 1831 – People 7,767,401.
Year 1841 – People 8,675,124.

So we're looking at nine million Irish people in Ireland in 1845. Many historians say it was between ten and twelve million in Ireland, one particular source says it was 14 million people in Ireland and they explain how some of the censuses are incorrect, given by authority to keep the numbers down. But lets even go with nine million Irish people in Ireland. Not everyone was registered and on the books.

We have been lied to. This is arguably one of the biggest lies in history. When I was in school, they taught us about the Irish famine, that we lived off potatoes and there was a potato blight and 1.5 million died and many emigrated. This was the official story from my history teacher who was Irish! She may have believed it but the truth needs to be exposed for it will haunt the psyche of Irish people from generation to generation forevermore, until the darkness becomes light.

There are eight-year-old kids in schools now asking, why couldn't the Irish people eat the fish, Ireland is surrounded by oceans? The lie cannot be covered up any longer, no matter how heart-wrenching it may be. The fishing boats were confiscated, mills for making flour, burnt down and grinding wheels broken.

Before we continue, you must first ask yourself two very important questions. Who wrote history? Why did they write history?

The answers to the questions are the British Empire wrote their take on history from their point of view, a self-congratulatory version of a colonial viewpoint at variance with the facts. They wrote the history books and within this chapter, you'll get to see why. What they did was quite cleverly done but covering up atrocity after atrocity.

Let's start off with the Potato blight. There was such a thing; it spread from America in 1844 to Europe, to England and one year later, to Ireland in 1845.

Ireland was abundant with food sources. Ireland had that much food such as bacon, pork, ham, eggs, barrels of oats, bags of flour, cattle, sheep and an abundant amount of seafood, not to mention the eight-year-olds question of surrounding oceans of fish.

At the time of the 'famine', there was enough food in Ireland to feed 18,000,000 people. It was the best country in Europe for growing, harvesting, and farming.

There were British soldiers all over Ireland at this time and when England found out that there was a Potato blight in their land, the British Establishment decided to start taking the food out of Ireland.

When the European potato crop failed in 1844 and food prices rose, Britain ordered regiments to Ireland. It's recorded by the Times editorial 30/Sept/1845 that the English people were having two meals a day that consisted of potatoes. England was highly overpopulated relative to the food supply the country had. It's correct to say that England faced the famine, not Ireland. Before the famine, before the potato blight even hit Ireland, British regiments were already sent to Ireland to take the food.

200,000 armed soldiers came to Ireland and held the Irish people at gunpoint and took their food. British landlords, called Irish landlords by Britain were sending all the food out. Irish people were held at gunpoint as they worried about how to feed their kids.

Ireland was exporting food to England at that time. This operation was part of the Tudor conquest that was going on in Ireland. There was an abundance of food in Ireland.

12,000 ships came from England to Ireland and a total of 200,000 British soldiers. There were 100,000 soldiers in Ireland at any given moment, whilst the rest was shipping tens of millions of livestock, grains, flour, meat, poultry and dairy products, enough food to feed a good portion of english people.

They did this for three reasons.

So England does not have a famine. They took so much more than they ever needed for profit. The British establishment tried to wipe out the Celtic people of Ireland in now what is known as genocide.

The real reason Ireland starved was that its food, from about 55 shiploads a day was removed at gunpoint by 12,000 British constables reinforced by the British militia, battleships, excise vessels, coast guards and by 200,000 British soldiers. If you would like to look into this further, check out www.irishholocaust.org

This is all recorded in the public record office London and has been copied by many people in case it goes missing, which conveniently has happened to the records of the British regiments daily activity records of 1845 – 1850.

This was only the start of this Genocide. Research has shown that there was really a population of over 10.5million in the census of 1841 in Ireland. There was a greater number in 1845. In the 1851 census recorded a population of 6.5million. Between the years 1845 – 1850 between 4 million to 6 million Irish people vanished.

The information that's given is, 100,000 Irish people fled to Canada in 1847 and only 60,000 survived. Many who got on the 'Coffin ships' and went to Liverpool did not survive the journey. Many immigrated to America and Australia. If 1 million immigrated, the other 3 to 5 Million are in mass graves around Ireland and also many died in the oceans surrounding Ireland.

And the painstaking truth is, there are many mass graves all over Ireland, perhaps as many as 3000 and the whereabouts of all these mass graves have been uncovered by the irishholocaust.org. Also there are mass graves in Canada and Australia.

Irish people, robbed of the food, thrown out of houses, many were murdered and mass graves all over Ireland tell the shocking truth of what really happened in Ireland – during our Great Hunger which sadly is known throughout the world that we had a potato famine and some died, some immigrated. It's an untrue story and if believed, it's a false belief.

The Coffin ships were old warships belonging to the British Empire. They were in wreck and ruin and the Irish were told that the Brits would immigrate the Irish to other countries.

Once the Coffin ships sailed out to sea, full of Irish people who had no choice but to leave Ireland, no food, no homes and dying, the British establishment sank the ships out at sea – after they collected their fair to travel to the new world.

Ireland is not the only country where the British establishment exercised this psychopath skill of theirs. I've worked in the desert land in Western Australia on and off for three years and the Aboriginal tribe made me part of their tribe (family) during my time up there. Really lovely people.

227 years of genocide and eviction. Places like Tasmania, which is an island bigger than Ireland – the whole area, combed by soldiers of the British army. Every Aboriginal man, woman, and child were slaughtered on their path and the rest were driven off the island and killed in the

oceans around it and some escaped to an island off Tasmania but later died. No Aboriginal person survived the British establishment's psychopathic skills of ridding the rightful owners of their land.

Tasmania is bigger than Ireland; the Aboriginal people are the longest surviving tribes in the world and are the longest surviving race of people on the same land as they have been in Australia for 77,000 years!

The Genocide continued all over Australia. It wasn't up until 1960 that the Aboriginal people started to get some recognition. Up until that time, an Aboriginal person could be shot and killed without breaking any laws, same as a Kangaroo can be shot and killed. Kangaroos are classed as vermin and up until 1960 Aboriginals were classed as vermin.

There are no exact figures of how many Aboriginal people were killed. History tells you there were about 1 million indigenous Australians and now 410,000. They lived in separate tribes, not just living off the land but traveling around the continent to sacred places all over Australia. They traded plants, food, hunting skills, the wisdom of the land and shared their spiritual understanding called Dreamtime stories, with each other. It's recorded now that there were 700 different languages spoken throughout Australia. They also built large dome shaped homes and were on this continent, Australia for 77,000 years.

In Ireland, the population of about 7 million people went up approx. 1 million every decade after the genocides and slavery stopped. Quick question? Looking at a different perspective. How many indigenous people do you think were living in Australia, 109 times the size of Ireland, left alone for thousands of years, never taken as slaves, zero genocides before their country was stolen? There are shadows of people walking this earth, wondering where the hell did the evil come from and now they're getting converted to Roman Catholic and Anglican Religions, so their questions can be answered. The cycle continues, history repeats itself until changed.

The indigenous people of Australia, awakened, educated, tribes, traveled all around Australia living off the land in groups. Dating back 77,000 years and their spiritual understanding is called Dreamtime, which recently has been discovered by scientists, that it's real.

Since the British establishment came to Australia with Irish slaves, some of the last tribes in the world lost their enlightened culture, many of them wiped out, the rest are feeling the pain passed on from generation to generation and many of them have to take drugs or drink to keep that pain bottled down and get out of their minds, before their own psyche wipes them out. Irish and Aboriginals get on very well – for we have a lot in common, regarding entertainment, music, the craic and are all subjected to the Brit's business model.

I've many Aboriginal friends still in with their tribes and they are great people, really amazing, friendly, kindhearted, warm people. You'll see other Aboriginals in the cities, attempting to adjust, from tribal culture to western civilisation, still great people, but some are broken and disconnected and some are sniffing petrol, paint thinners, drinking alcohol when they have money, many people judge them from the first glance, but in reality, they are broken people and they need to do these things to survive the hell on earth their grandparents went through, the tribes that are lost, the lost generation and what they are going through today, their culture, their Dreamtime all stolen. And this is very similar to areas of the Irish population, only it seems worse in Ireland with the suicides.

The only way for the Celts and the Aboriginals to heal from this, is to make the darkness conscious, to bring light to what happened, otherwise, the pain gets passed on from generation by energy in motion (emotions) and eventually if the darkness stays in the dark, swept under the carpet, that pain will wipe out the remaining Legends of the Tribes around the World.

We are losing populations with true knowledge of the land, true wisdom of themselves and understanding of how the Universe works on both sides of the world. Then the ones who survive, culture stolen, mushroomized and then fed Roman Catholic religion and Protestant Methodist Norman Anglican for answers.

The Aboriginal people of Australia dropped from 1 million (according to history books) to 100,000 in the first century after the invasion in 1788.

Tasmania Aboriginal people dropped from 60,000 (according to history – a place bigger than Ireland) to zero from the years 1776 – 1803.

And the Maori population dropped from 200,000 in 1800 to 42,000 in 1893.

Genocide is what the Queen ordered in almost every country that the British establishment invaded, including Ireland. In other countries, it was invasion and slaughter. In Ireland, they pretended to be our friends; our allies and they stole our food and executed us. This genocide, is what they did, worldwide.

There's a name for this type of person or organisation who holds these traits and it's called a psychopath. Wikipedia says 'Psychopaths are rational and aware of what they are doing and why. Their behaviour is the result of choice, freely expressed. They have impaired empathy and remorse and bold, disinhibited, egotistical traits.'

In the last century, a government repented and paid out $100 Billion Dollars to the Jews. Ireland deserves one serious payout for all the genocides caused there.

Quick history lesson

1701 – Catholics banned from the throne. 1714, Queen Anne died. Her 50 or so closest suitable relatives were all Catholic, so that wouldn't work for them. George was Anne's closest living Protestant relative.

George Ludwig, the Protestant prince-elector of Hanover (Germany) got the job but he didn't speak much English so his ministers had to run Britain for him.

He was called George 1st and he was King of Great Britain and Ireland. Did you know we had a German King who not only ruled our land but also didn't speak any English never mind any Irish?

Then we have the Jacobites who tried to depose George 1st and replace with Anne's Catholic half brother James Stuart but it was a failed attempt. The Jacobites were an army of French, Scottish and had 700 Irish volunteers in the group. George 2nd and 3rd, still a Hanoverian but could speak English as a first language.

1819, Queen Victoria marries her German cousin Albert. The Royal family didn't use surnames; they only used first names and the property name. The Royal house changed from Stuart to Brunswick-Lüneburg-Hanover, bringing with it a wealth of connections to the ancient royal houses of Welf; and Este, which is the parent house, all owned by Germany and Italy and UK. Henry VIII was a Tudor, George I was a Hanover.

When WWI bred increasing anti-German sentiment in Britain – they realised that Kaiser Bill was not only King George V's first cousin but also Queen Victoria's grandson. It was a delicate situation for them, so George V changed the name of his Royal house from Saxe-Coburg-Gotha to Windsor after the castle and took the modern step of adopting Windsor as a surname for his family.

The Royal family has genetic and cultural ties with the people of Germany for over 1500 years. 1952, Queen Elizabeth, as Philips wife should adopt his name – Mountbatten, but she continued with the house of Windsor. Long live the Windsor's – not my circus, not my monkeys — but what a show!

After they drove the Irish out of our country, killed most Irish on the journey, the rest absolutely starving, they wrote in the American papers, 'drunks and dogs'. Who ran the country then? The British Empire.

The Irish were called Dogs and treated worse than you would ever treat a dog. As were the North American Indian. The Brits made out in American newspapers that the Irish are dogs, meaning a dog eat dog world. Their intentions were to make us turn on each other and fulfil the dog eat dog term but we didn't, no matter what they did to us or how much they starved us, the Irish hung in there and looked after one another and each area they went to, they started from scratch and showed their skills and built places, the Irish not only made the plans for the White House in America, but built it.

You see, we do not see things as they are – we see them as — we are. Nobody is doing anything wrong given their model of the world, their education, their life experiences, each mind works of rational thought, no one person, is to blame for every action is justified in one's mind, by rational thinking. The foundation of some organisations and even individuals comes down to three types of people, people with empathy, narcissistic people and psychopaths, each making rational decisions based on their inner drive or impaired sense of being a human being.

So, the solution is not war, but rather understanding of events, and perhaps helping evolve these organisations into human beings some day, with empathy and understanding. History can help us achieve levels of compassion.

Tony Blair recently made an apology about the 'famine'.

CHAPTER 7

100 years ago - 1916 Rising.

Many people in Ireland knew that Britain perpetrated a Holocaust in Ireland and they wanted Britain to stop killing Irish people, so a rising started.

The lack of education for many Irish in the 20th century and even today, is a Policy by the British Empire.

We, a people of scientists, inventors, discoverers, philosophers, engineers, musicians, poets, tradespeople and artists, decided enough was just enough and took on the British Empire, an Empire that nearly owned the world, and we won. We Won! This should be the most significant paragraph in the book as our forefathers paved the way for Aiden, India, Cypris, and Egypt and others of the British Empire to look for independence.

Our forefathers came together proclaiming enough is enough, and Ireland became almost whole again. Our forefathers took on the British Empire, and we won our right to liberty.

There is a reason why they've thieved our Northern Ireland. Not to mention the gold they are currently sifting out of it.

Also, Catholics and Protestants wanted a republic, so the British Empire caused a civil war in Ireland. If interested in knowing more about that — you'll have to Read James Plunket and Farewell Companions.

Basically, Britain wanted a civil war to turn Ireland upside down. Éamon de Valera (Dev) knew, so he hurried it up to get it over with. The only cards on the table were, either send the country into civil war that would never recover from – or a nation divided into five or six states, or Dev's best move was just hurry it up and get it over with so the next generation could have useful lives.

The Irish civil war took place between two parties. The new Irish government backed by most of the Dáil, and the anti-treaty men, under the leadership of Dev against the pro-treaty Free State forces. This went on from June 1922 to May 1923.

Both sides wanted to avoid civil war, but fighting broke out over the takeover of the Four Courts building in Dublin by anti-Treaty members of the IRA. Michael Collins was forced to act against them when Winston Churchill threatened to re-occupy the country with British troops unless action was taken.

Did you know Dev, who was also a mathematician and Einstein were friends? Really bright people who could not only see the bigger picture but had a great understanding of the overall solutions. Dev wanted to rebuild Dublin with fields on the outside where it grows its own food, around the city, has its own food supply; the man was ahead of his time.

The IRA was the resistance against the British Empire stealing our land, our people and wiping us out for 750 years.

The British Empire had ownership of that much land around the world that the Sun never set on it. In 1913 the British Empire held sway over 412 million people. At its height, it was the largest Empire in history with ownership of a landmass of 35,500,000 kms.

Ireland has a landmass of 84,421 kms. Ireland took on the British Empire for human dignity and freedom and brought murdering savagery of the British Empire to an end and paved the way for other prisoner countries to strike for freedom too.

Did you know, ancient healers and visionaries of Ancient Ireland were put on the streets and became travellers. They were psychics, mediums, practitioners, visionary's and teachers of their communities. This is what made us free from the control and power forces for so long, as we could foresee events.

The British Empire came in and put our educational leaders on the streets in order to put our country on its knees, to destroy the intelligent power we had, to break a population. The resistance, that's not recognised today.

The British establishment said when they're preaching their victory about history. "A Celt will soon be as rare on the banks of the Shannon as the Red Man on the banks of Manhattan."

There's a quote by Dan Breen on killing Black and Tans – "Yes I killed them, all killing is murder to me. I make no apologies for killing, and the only thing that I was ever really sorry for was the number that escaped."

I only heard about Dan Breen for the first time this year, as we were not taught about the war of independence in school. Breen, Sean Tracey, and Tom Barry, to name a few, are not given credit due to them by the state. Very few people today have a clue about what these heroes did for our country. This is what Irish had to do to defend the country.

Killing is never good but killing diseased, criminally insane killers to save millions of innocent lives, in the cause of liberating one's country from oppression then, it had to be done. Theobald Wolfe Tone knew he was fighting a losing battle, Pearce knew it too, but they opposed because they believed in another generation.

Wolfe Tone who was the revolutionist of 1798 rebellion said, "Our independence must be had at all hazards if the men of property will not support us, they must fall, we can support ourselves by the aid of that numerous and respectable class of the community – the men of no property."

Wolfe Tone also said, 'To subvert the tyranny of our execrable government, to break the connection with England, the never-failing source of all our political evils and to assert the independence of my country – these were my objectives."

But, I'll repeat this, the problem is not the English people we know today, many too now see their governments antics.

When Hitler rose, some Irish helped the English. Dev and many Irish were happy to leave England to their own devices, which was very understandable but the English asked for help, and some Irish did, as they saw a bigger Tyrant in Hitler. You see, England would have been in big trouble if Hitler got into Ireland, (the back door to the Empire) removed British troops from Northern Ireland, leaving the Brits nowhere to run and attacked from both sides of the British Isles. There was a plan for Hitler to get into Ireland called operation Green – IRA changed the name to operation Kathleen – an Irish version of operation Green.

Hitler's views about operation Green should be by invitation only by Irish. Hitler said, "..a landing in Ireland can be attempted only if Ireland requests help. The occupation of Ireland might lead to the end of the war. First, we must ascertain whether De Valera desires to support."

After the war, the English lads, who lost friends and saw limbs ripped apart wanted to come back to England and have a rebellion. Churchill sent the English soldiers from London up to Scotland and many Scots down to London to move them around, so that no such rebellion occurs.

The English soldiers and the Irish soldiers got on well, as the English soldiers could see what was really going on when involved in English wars outside the politics of England. So, there you go.

CHAPTER 8

Northern Ireland

I just saw on the Internet, it was a windup, but it had me going for a while and it said….

June 29 – 2016 The Queen officially hands Northern Ireland back to Ireland. The 90-year-old monarch thanked the people of Northern Ireland for remaining under British rule for so long and apologised to their republic counterparts for all the atrocities over the past 70 years.

"Our proud nations have been through thick and thin together," "So forgive me if I appear a little emotional, it has been a long road for everyone here. It is my honour to hand over the six Counties, Antrim, Armagh, Down, Fermanagh, Londonderry, Tyrone, and all its financial woes over to the Republic of Ireland." The Queen said.

Financial woes! Woe means, grievous distress, affliction, or trouble. Example; His woe was almost beyond description.

Ireland is the food basket for England. England colonised America, but America became independent in 1776. England has Australia, but a lot of Australia is desert land. Ireland has always been the most fertile land and the food basket for England.

The Queen was going to give Northern Ireland back in 1970, but Ireland wanted 13 Billion Punts, on damages to fix the North. 60's in the North were just terrible. They were just ignored due to zero media coverage coming out of the place and so much damage happened where the psyche may never recover. Irish were moving out of the North to the South as their houses were getting burnt to the ground.

During 1969, Northern Ireland was rocked by intense political and sectarian rioting. There had been a lot of violence throughout the year arising from the civil rights campaign, which was demanding an end to discrimination against Irish Catholics.

Civil rights marches were repeatedly attacked by Protestant Loyalists and by the Royal Ulster Constabulary. The disorder led to the Battle of the Bogside in Derry, a three-day riot in the district between the RUC and the nationalist, the Irish residents.

The British Army was deployed to restore order and control, and peace lines began to be built to separate the two sides. The events of August 1969 are widely seen as the beginning of the thirty-year conflict known as 'The Troubles'.

It was a complete fabrication to England. Religion was to suit England, our land, money – our own food supply – everything was a fabrication to England.

H-Blocks were like concentration camps. Set up in 1976 for Irish people fighting for their rights on their own land. When internment was introduced, it was directed against true Irishmen to house prisoners during the Troubles from 1971 to 2000.

It was situated southwest of Belfast. Seven prisoners went on hunger strike. Margaret Thatcher appeared to concede to their demands, but she didn't in the end. So another hunger strike took place in 1981. Sands died 66 days later, and another 9 died in the hunger strike. 100,000 people attended Sands funeral in Belfast and another 9 were to die in the hunger strike. Sands was elected as MP, a month before he died in prison and nearly every city in France and many places in the world have a street named after Bobby Sands. Thatcher never recovered from that.

In 1983 – the H-Block Maze saw the most significant breakout. Thirty-eight prisoners hijacked a prison meals lorry and smashed their way out. It was shut down in 2000.

It was incredible, a torture camp for Irish people on their own land, some movies are coming out about it now and some videos on YouTube, but I believe the real story has never been told yet! 54,000 Irish people are driven out of Northern Ireland in 1969 – Irish refugees in Ireland – Crazy!

What I'm writing is only pointers to the true Irish history. Internment was a torturing concentration camp where any real Irish person was a victim. The way the arrests were carried out and the abuse of those arrested led to mass protests. 7000 people fled or were forced out of their homes. The European Commission of Human rights described the interrogation techniques used in 1976 as torture and 1,981 people were locked up in there.

There was big security on the Northern Ireland border, one must ask themselves the question, why is it there? Then you have the Republic Irish border, a toilet and one security man, which is a statement 'extracting the urine' out of the need to have security there.

Lord Mountbatten was a British statesman and naval officer, an uncle of Prince Philip, Duke of Edinburgh and second cousin once removed to Elizabeth II. He came over to holiday in Ireland and was always asking, is there people here belonging to the IRA. He was told many times not to say that or carry on that way, but he didn't stop, and he put his family in danger. In 1979, the IRA – put a bomb in his fishing boat, in County Sligo, blew up Mountbatten, his grandson Nicholas and two others.

So the queen, shedding a few tears, red-faced and saying, "Our proud nations have been through thick and thin together." Doesn't quite cut it. She needs to be accountable for giving it back. We never gave it in the first place – tooth and nail to hang onto it and many died in the process. Who's going to pay for the damages? It could be 50 years before that place gets fixed. They should be coughing up 30 Billion plus for damages in Northern Ireland alone.

The whole of Britain's involvement in Ireland is an unimaginable scale of Genocide. The British Empire lives in a delusion of property and grandeur and has little or no respect for human life.

There was the Good Friday agreement set up on April 10, 1998, a peace process for both the Irish Republic and unionists to sign. Both sides agreed in this peace process, but neither side signed it but achieved 15 years of peace, something that was never imagined possible.

In Nothern Ireland, there is a yearly Ulster protestant Celebration on the 11th night of July, before their Orange march on the 12th of July, which consists of bonfires, many reaching 100 foot tall. The flag of Ireland, Irish nationalist symbols, Catholic symbols, are burnt on many bonfires.

Let's look behind the scenes in this 21st century. What we have now is mining going on called open cut Gold mining estimated to be 11 Billion Euro's worth, to go on for the next 6 years at the Clontibert site, in County Monaghan on the British border in Ireland.

The are taking our Gold and the other problem is, they use mercury to Gold mine. Mercury destroys land and gives brain damage – destroys unborn children and destroys the soil, it also destroys the water, you can't get it out and it is one of the most deadly substances in the world. When you have mercury, damaged soil and water, the people using it become brain damaged and that becomes a long-term serious problem for the country.

Open cut mining took place in Australia, the mining companies only care about getting the Gold or the minerals they are after, the mines fill up with rainwater, one mine overflowed recently and it spilled acid and heavy metals into the Dee river killing birds and fish. The water from the river can't be drunk anymore, it's aluminium poisoning that's wiping out the birds and fish even 55k's down the river. Many politicians say, "Thank god it didn't happen on our watch." But never the less, it's happening, and the people and government don't know how to fix the problem as it cost money they say. 15,000 abandoned mines in Queensland and 50,000 abandoned mines across the country.

It's happening at the Clontibert site, in County Monaghan on the Irish border as of now 2018 as I'm writing this.

And it's important to realise, regarding possible freedom for Ireland and for the health and wealth of the Irish legends,

Whomever has the Gold, makes the rules!

CHAPTER 9

The Celtic Tiger, The Recession & Tribes.

All that lending of money and then taking your house, your land and perhaps your country – it's an old trick.

Too much was happening to the Irish, the rest of Europe stepped in and told England, enough, just stop, it's too much for any country to take. We had a Celtic Roar, from the Celtic Tiger and Vibe by Vibe, we moved into Elevation.

Banks were giving out 100% loans, so you didn't need any money to buy a house, and house prices just kept going up and up, so you got one or four, even just thinking that you could sell it the next day for an extra 50K.

Sessions galore all over Ireland – finally something good has happened to Ireland, and everyone was minted. But people wanted more and more, setting themselves up for retirement and their grandkids retirement. Greed kicked in when all you really needed was money (energy) and Elán, and there would have been no stopping the country.

Australia

While lads at home had the Celtic Roar, I was working in the desert 14,000k's from Ireland and 4,000k's from my family home in Australia. Building houses for my Aboriginal Aussie friends funded by the Australian government. I always played music up there, and when around the Aboriginals - I was asked to download and play Irish singers.

Let's talk about the Aboriginal's of Australia. So I played Irish music, that I never heard before, all of them love music but more so, the Irish singers, they said we were the best. I never saw anything like it – singing and dancing to Irish music. I felt like I found a new home in the desert with absolute Legends – who were teaching me about our Irish singers that I never heard of. I was totally mind blown and privileged to be the Irish man to bring this celebration to the desert land.

If you would like to see volumes about the Aboriginals struggle – watch 'Rabbit-Proof Fence' – the movie and a show on TV called First Contact. Very interesting as the same doctrine was used in Ireland – different structure though.

Aboriginals say Paul Kelly sang them a song called 'From Little Things, Big Things Grow.' The Aboriginals of Australia are drawing maps of the sky at night – the dots on their paintings are of stars and planets. Papunya art consists of various paint colour's like yellow (representing the Sun), brown (the soil), red (desert land) and white (clouds in the sky). Also, they have Dreamtime, which consists of many ancient stories of the Milky Way and the seven sisters and spirals in the skies. I personally think they are the last tribes on this planet that really know what's going on. The Australian Aboriginal is arguably the most successful and indeed the most extended surviving culture in human history.

Any fighting they ever had in history was Tribal fights with one another, with fist fighting and perhaps spears. They never saw guns, nor invented such deadly weapons to harm one another. It was really an advanced civilisation in many ways, as they shared the land and their Dreamtime stories, they had respect for each other, the culture, many different tribes traveled around sharing the same territory in peace and harmony. They were not prepared for what came to their lands and still they don't wish to fight back, only live inland away in some sort of peace and harmony. They only try team up now to protect the land and rivers from mining and protect sacred land that's getting stolen. They just want to be classed as people, and they are working on keeping their culture alive - all tribes are getting connected now through technology. They call each other Mobs now instead of a tribe with a great sense of humour to it. They are passionate, they are funny, they are deep and they hold wisdom that the white man (Brit establishment) could not possibly comprehend and a lot of it is to do with planets and stars, ancient understanding, plus it's their culture and should only be explained in person, by invite only. They are a great tribe of people, with compassion and empathy like no other tribe before and are the longest surviving race in the world.

Ireland

Back to Ireland, the recession at Ireland – the best thing that came out of the recession, was that Irish got together to help each other out. The greed had faded away, and we were left with a less material world, once down to our core, people were helping people, caring for each other and overall, it was a beautiful thing to hear.

People are generally good you know, and people all over the world want happiness and the good things in life, friends, trusting relationships, loyalty, a good laugh, some compassion, connection with others and to spend good times with their families – to enjoy life.

Authority wrote history, many people in England have been programmed to believe it's the greatest country in the world. It's a program of education that only consists of false knowledge, propaganda and false beliefs.

I've met people from Iran; they respected us Irish lads, because we're Irish and they knew more about Irish history than I did. But they had respect for us, they said, 'you're like us, defending ourselves against the British Empire.' We, Irish, have max respect from people around the world who know our history. But no one knows why it all happened? Because no one knows about our New Grange apart from the Empires that tried to bury it and steal the power, but their stolen power is false, the foundation of it all is at our site, New Grange - the most loving, source connecting, place on Earth.

It's the powers that are the ones that are causing havoc in our world these days. Can you see that? There are about 7 billion people in the world and there are about 3 thousand people running the show, mainly narcissistic sadistic people and we're driven to hate each other, divided into groups, taught false history and separation on almost every level imaginable.

Money

Let's go back to this illusion of money. 3 trillion dollars, the Earth owes on money, to whom? They lend you money that does not exist, the banks lend nine times the amount they actually have, and then they'll take your house, your land, your wife, your country – it's an old trick. History repeats itself until changed.

You see, Gold is the real currency; it doesn't decrease in value, as an ounce of Gold equals an ounce of Gold, no matter what country you are in.

The Gold is getting, continually stolen, taken from all countries, by those String Masters - those in power. It's all still here on the Earth! Gold is only formed from a Star exploding, it's called a Super Nova, and the Gold stays around forever. Gold is the answer to currency problems worldwide – and the String Masters are the 21st-century problem.

You might not understand this – but let me just say – Ireland is a Slave Shop and Australia is an Open Prison.

One of the illusions is, people don't see they are becoming slaves, too busy working every day, getting paid half a wage of an illusion called paper money, that they give to the banks or who never had the money in the first place to lend and get back the interest on top. Whilst working and paying for our own houses we built ourselves and for electricity we discovered ourselves and the water that falls from the sky above us, almost every day!

You see, when you're in Plato's cave, you don't know there's a cave. When you travel and step outside Plato's cave, you see old friends stuck in the same cave you just got out of. When you move out of a town, you get to see things from a bigger perspective. When you move out of the country and travel the world and meet the people of the world and listen to their amazing insights into Ireland that you don't usually see or hear of and when you travel that many countries and speak to that many people about their country, your perspective and listen to their view of your country, you start to see a picture, one that is well beyond the Plato cave I grew up in, it's very educational.

Let's look at Ireland – you know how vital Ireland is, apart from the Spiritually that exists there – it's an essential part of Europe – it's a landing base for America, it's on the edge of Europe and for some reason, it never really gets conquered! Ireland has mountains on the outside – water on the inside – it is the most fertile land on the planet the Green land.

Erin Gó Bragh!

CHAPTER 10

Resilience

L et's start with the Irish Fans — These Legends deserve a mention; did you ever see such a kind, powerful, full of empathy, singing, chanting, dancing, group of people, in all your life? The Irish Fans are the only Fans in the world, who's Fan's have Fans! There is a rare gene, only found within the DNA of the Celt, it's called Irish Endurance; still, they have not broken our resilience. The Irish Celt lives!

The Irish Fans show Irish Endurance, still, even after all we have been through, we still come from a place of genuine love, of kindness, demonstrating compassion to fellow foreign individuals and authority, singing and dancing, that is who we are and have always been, entertainers and peace keepers. The Irish Fans, the people of Ireland, should be the leaders of Ireland and not a continuous chain of murdering, thieving, corrupt politicians whose only purpose is to utterly annihilate the country and its people, on their Quest for a Knighthood!

Approx 40% of Australians are Irish descent. Irish were taken as slaves. History will tell you they were convicts. They were hard-working family men who are trying to feed their own families, with food that they grew themselves, were called 'convicts' according to the Queen. (brit establishment)

71

Australia was not an easy country to grow up in with snakes and killer spiders not to mention the fighting Kangaroos and that was the easy part, the Union Jack flag men killed anyone who stepped out of their strict control, our in-laws, our out-laws, our aboriginal legend friends, basically any civilised, evolved, compassionate, tribal people under the stranglehold, were beaten badly or slaughtered, Irish are hardcore, so many survived.

Now we have a heap of Aussie's who are like long lost cousins and love the Irish. The Aboriginals have similarities as they experienced the same colonisation and doctrine and to my amazement, they love Irish music, its more passionate, so they insist.

The Resilience comes in for the Irish Legends when we understand Irish History. Most of the discoveries and inventions we read in our British history books has happened already. Look at the wheel for example – we didn't realise that it was already discovered by us, along with the discovery of America and Canada and inventing electricity! But let's do a little summary on the centuries of Ireland from last Millennia to soak in the resilience.

We are minding our own business in Ireland, having a great time, having the Craic, creating books like the book of Durrow, book of Armagh and the book of Kells, making masterpieces, with agriculture drawings for amazing structures, growing foods in the most extensive farming ways and celebrating by singing songs and dancing, telling great stories to our grandkids and having celebrations around the heart of Ireland, Hill of Tara, Slane and New Grange. This was a really civilised advanced society, whilst a few of our Kings were having one or two punch-ups every so often, just to keep the hearts ticking, nothing too serious, a bit of Craic.

Then these Vikings came in, from 800 to 1169, we had Viking raids followed by the Norman invasions. Instead of New Grange being our capital along with the Hill of Tara, towns were set up called Dublin, Wexford, Waterford, Cork, and Limerick with the Vikings.

There were independent, civilised tribes in Ireland called the Túath. They were based in the countryside and consisted of dwellings ranging from 3000 – 9000 people. Life was so good in Ireland, as the people are amazing and we were living off the most fertile land in the world in a very advanced tribal community, with all the people looking after each other as one community, and educating each other to reach higher levels of evolution and consciousness. The dream was a reality.

Whilst the invasions happened, many attempts were made by various tribes to take over the whole island to protect Ireland and its people. The Uí Néill's ran the show for centuries but there was a conflict between the Northern and Southern branches which caused a weakness. Brian Boru came along, loved by the people and became the first High King of Ireland, that was not part of the Uí Néill's family clan for centuries.

In Ireland at this stage, there were about a million people who in total had about 150 Kings, and Brian became the High King of Ireland during his reign from 1002 – 1014.

The Norman invasion of the late 12th century marked the beginning of more than 750 years of direct British Empire rule in Ireland. In 1177, the Crown came up with a policy of plantation, involving the arrival of thousands of English and Scottish (Lowlands – English or Normans, who lived in Scotland) Protestant settlers, and removed the Irish Catholics from their land.

Protestant domination in Ireland was confirmed after two periods of war between Irish and Protestants in 1641-52 and 1689-91. Political power after this, became Protestant, while the Irish suffered severe political and economic privations under the Penal Laws.

The Irish Parliament was abolished from 1/January/1801 in the wake of the republican United Irishmen Rebellion and Ireland became an integral part of a new United Kingdom of Great Britain and Ireland, under provisions of the Acts of Union 1800.

The Irish Parliamentary party strove from the 1880s to attain Home Rule through the parliamentary constitutional movement, eventually winning the Home Rule Act 1914, although this Act was suspended at the outbreak of World War 1.

The Easter Rising occurred and brought back the Fighting Irish again. Philosophers, scientists, engineers, doctors, musicians, poets and ordinary Irish men and women got together and they took on the Empire and they beat the Empire! Wow!!

In 1922, after the Irish War of Independence and the Anglo-Irish Treaty, most of Ireland seceded from the United Kingdom to become the independent Irish Free State, which after the 1937 Constitution, began to call itself Ireland.

The six Northeastern counties, known as Northern Ireland, remained within the United Kingdom.

Our Irish legends were up against many laws and legislation that were put in place to keep the Irish Celts down over the centuries. Did you know the psychopaths who wear their three-piece suits, sipping tea, at tea parties, set up a statutory penalty in parliaments such as the 'Hung, Drawn & Quartered legislation in 1351 which went on till 1870 and the death penalty for treason was only abolished in 1998?

Well, it involved getting a person, hanging them until they are nearly dead but keeping them alive. Then cutting out their intestines, barbecuing it and putting it back into their bodies and sewing it up. Then getting four horses, tying the person's legs and arms to a rope to each horse and whipping the horses. Many English lads were convicted of high treason and the majority of victims were English and Irish Catholic priests.

The Penal Laws were set up by the psychopaths making ott laws and legislation to wipe out the people, designed for the destruction of a Race of People - known as The Celts.

The Penal laws were, according to Edmund Burke, "a machine of wise and elaborate contrivance, as well fitted for the oppression, impoverishment, degradation, and extermination of a people and the debasement in them of human nature itself, as ever proceeded from the perverted ingenuity of man."

Did you ever hear of the Black & Tans – Yes? It was Lloyd George, not Churchill who sent the Black and Tans to Ireland. They were temporary recruits, ex-cons, in July 1920, they added an Auxiliary division composed of, demobbed, out of work, Army officers. These men received no police training and were free from normal discipline and went about terrorising the country. Army officers were drawn from the upper class of English society at the time which makes their behaviour totally unacceptable. They knew what they were doing. Some of the Black and Tans were criminally insane people, from jails in England. TB and VD cause massive brain damage and was the first germ warfare transmitted by human to human as a war plan.

Ireland declared its independence from the UK in 1919. The Transition of Power happened in the Irish General Election of 1932. The 1937 constitution overseen by Eamon de Valera was to state that the whole of Ireland and its islands and surrounding oceans, are to be owned and run by the people of Ireland.

You know there were British soldiers in Ireland called 'Beef Eaters' – they protected the Queen and killed Irish landowners and got to keep the land for themselves.

Dispossessed Irish – Spoils of war it's called – we need to claim our land back.

Keating's visit to Ireland, he said something like, you fought the English Empire and won. You don't give yourself credit for that. India followed suit because of Ireland and Australia is a democracy because of Ireland. Irish set examples for other countries against the British Empire around the world.

We are the Gaels - Irish are total Legends – don't ever forget that.

The Irish flag was first used in 1848, Green White and Orange. Green for republic, white for peace, and orange for our brothers and sisters in the northern Ireland whom we cherish and love as one nation today.

Kilmainham Jail

Let's discuss our own Jail in Dublin called Kilmainham Gaol.

Kilmainham jail played a big part in Irish history and 1916 rising. The Irish who were fighting back in a desperate attempt to stop the atrocities continually happen in Ireland, imprisoned and shot dead.

James Connelly and the crew, all shot dead on our own land in Kilmainham Jail. There are still bullet holes in G.P.O in Dublin from 1916 and even today – 100 years later, there is still no real recognition for the Irish Legends of Ireland. No Inclusive History. Kilmainham Gaol, Dublin, Ireland.

The British Jails before that was in Spike Island, Clonmel Borstal, Geneva Barracks, Newgate Prison, Richmond, Sligo Goal, The Black Dog, Cork city Goal and Cork County Gaol.

Since independence, Ireland has enjoyed an extremely low rate of imprisonment in comparison with the rate when it was part of the United Kingdom.

Kilmainham Gaol is now a museum run by the Office of Public Works which is an agency of The government of Ireland.

Many Irish revolutionaries, including the Leaders of the 1916 Easter Rising, were imprisoned and executed in prison by the British.

There were many movies filmed at Kilmainham Gaol like The Whistle Blower, In the Name of the Father, Michael Collins, The Escapist, The Wind that Shakes the Barley and a U2 song called 'A Celebration'.

The Leaders & Legends that were all executed after Easter of 1916 – men who were just trying to give us a chance to live. P.H Pearse, Thomas J.Clarke and Thomas MacDonagh executed 3/May/1916. Joseph Plunkett, Edward Daly, Michael O'Hanrahan and William Pearse executed 4/May/1916. John MacBride executed 5/May/1916

Con Colbert, Èamonn Ceannt, Michael Mallin and Seán Heuston executed 8/May/1916. Seán Mac Diarmada and James Connolly executed 12/May/1916.

So, that's all, I would like to say maximum Respect to these men and woman who tried to pave the way for us to have some chance of living a happy, fulfilling life. Tiocfaidh ár lá!

Irish history is blow after blow after blow. We were subjugated and impoverished by the Brits, but we never gave up. We have an excellent understanding for others in that same situation and have made a significant contribution to Trade unions, education, civil rights work, medical and all avenues. Now we have an understanding of people, all around the world as no other nation in history has taken as many blows as us and still, we stand - Proud as the Irish Legends.

It wasn't so long ago, we had to survive under the radar - couldn't speak of Ireland, or speak our language, or do our Irish dancing, so we talk of Rosìn or Kathleen as Ireland, couldn't carry arms, so we use the Blackthorn, couldn't play Bagpipes, so we invented Uileann pipes. Couldn't have St Brigid's cross so used the theology hidden in the grass. Resilient inventive.

From little things - big things grow. But first, do we really own Ireland? Who owns all the commercial shops in Dublin? Are owned by Irish or owned by foreigners in our country?

You see, in Ireland in 1922, the Brits owned the real estate. They set up false documents, saying that they hold the lease for 50 years. So, Ireland, although got most of the country back – still didn't have ownership. It was to be in 1972 before Irish could repurchase the real estate. The deal was for Irish to own it then after the fifty-year lease. But what happened then? Well, the Brits had children who were born in Ireland, thus are Irish and they just inherited it – so we still own very little indeed. And the landlords of many properties today are all working in the Dáil. Brits still want Ireland and are taking it, until we wake up!

The country could be on its way with the oil findings alone not to mention all the Gold in the mines on the border of Northern Ireland, Monaghan – but Ireland is getting stolen from top to bottom to this day.

You want to see how to get Northern Ireland back? Aboriginals are well on their way with land rights. You play the game, play by the rules of the system. It's called Land rights.

Aussie Eddie Koiki Mabo – An Aboriginal man who just wanted to bury his father on his own land up North in Australia. He wasn't allowed. It was land taken by the British – men holding a Union Jack Flag. A big thing happened as Eddie wasn't giving up, as he had a lot of respect for his father.

Eddie was able to show the Australian government a painting from a thousand years ago, showing the ground, tree, the stones and Aboriginal people in the painting, which showed the property was Eddie's families land before stolen.

It sparked off a lot of stuff as it cut more profoundly than the Brit establishment core. Eddie Koiki Mabo got to bury his father on his own land. Land rights.

If we wanted, we could get our land back through the system – without any forms of harmful violence – we could have back Northern Ireland

and our surrounding Islands and oceans and fulfil Ireland yet again –
The way it should be as intended in the 1937 Constitution and a Salute
to Dev.

The Wolf Tones – who got their name from the Irish rebel and patriot
Theobald Wolfe Tone – one of the leaders of the Irish Rebellion of 1798
later went to release "You'll Never beat the Irish."

Also, an historical message engraved in stone in one of our Celtic
nations called Britannia says 'Rather death than dishonour - our land
of our fathers - the Celts'.

Resilience and Le grá mór.

CHAPTER 11

Iʀísb Enɒuʀɑnce

My sister in Ireland told me, 'One does not become enlightened by imagining figures of light – the only way we are to evolve as an Island is to make the darkness conscious,' and that's what we're doing here.

You know everyone in Ireland says, sorry this and sorry that. 'Sorry I have a drug problem,' 'ah, sorry to hear about that.'

Nothing is our fault – we have done nothing wrong – we've just been broken that many times and our psyche is affected because it's getting past on from generation to generation.

We are sorry because we don't know what we are doing wrong, yet we want this all to stop, but none of it is our fault, so let's not be victims, lets rise above victimhood – darkness to light – and let's wake up.

Here we have a list of all hated men in Ireland. Shortened up with what they did.

Oliver Cromwell – He murdered and deported tens of thousands of Irish as slaves. (a Brit)

Diarmuid Mac Murrough – King Henry was just waiting for an opening and hell on earth began, and the Irish have been trying to get rid of them ever since. (a Stitch up)

William Trevelyan – Britain's overseer of Ireland during the Great Hunger. Wiped out so many Irish people and mass graves are all over Ireland and in the surrounding Oceans. (Brit Establishment)

Lord Lucan – The worse landlord in Ireland during the Great Hunger. He turned 10,000 people out of their homes in Ballinrobe in Mayo alone. (Brit Establishment)

Captain William O'Shea – The resulting Victorian era scandal took down Ireland's 'Uncrowned King.'
(a Brit army man and his wife was English)

David Lloyd George – Also known as the Welsh Wizard, he split the Irish delegation during the treaty talks and insisted on Irish partition and keeping his unionist backers happy at all costs. (Born in Manchester, England)

Winston Churchill – He invented the Black and Tans and Lloyd George sent them to Ireland to force surrender. (Brit's)

General Eoin O'Duffy – He was an admirer of Hitler. In the 1930's he started the 'Blueshirts' which was the Irish equivalent of the Nazis. (Brit Establishment)

Margaret Thatcher, – She allowed the IRA prisoners, led by Bobby Sands, to starve to death in 1981. The move backfired when Sands elected as MP and kick-started the Sinn Fein political rise before he died. (She was born – Westminster London, worked for the Brit establishment)

Cornel Derek Wilford – He gave the order to fire on unarmed civilians on 'Bloody Sunday.' Twenty-six were shot, and 14 died. Subsequently known as 'the Butcher of the Bogside.'
(a British Army Officer – with zero remorse)

Bertie Aherne – destroyed thousands of Irish lives. Running for office again. (Irish man) Is this really the best we can do?

Enda Kenny – has led a government that has overseen the mass evictions of thousands of Irish families from their homes. He has watched as the homelessness problems have worsened while at the same time enriched the already fabulously wealthy and is currently on his Quest for a Knighthood! (A Puppet)

Brian Cowen – coincide with the Irish financial and banking crises. Had to request for a financial rescue from the EU and the IMF widely seen in Ireland as a national humiliation. Irish Independent called Cowen the "worse Taoiseach in the history of the State." (Irish Clown)

And there we have The British Queen – who has never accepted an interview in the history of the world.

We have been, invaded, degraded, famished, murdered, taken by Genocide, received acts of total savagery, beyond terrorism and when a group of us fight back, we're branded the terrorists. We have been outcasted, enslaved, exiled, beaten, worn and torn, muppetized, mushroomized and still, We are a proud people, known throughout the world as the Irish Legends. And hopefully someday - The Awakening of the Celts!

One of the greatest endurance today is, when you get told history, it will mess you up. When you look into our history, it will really mess you up, and you can't seem to get to the core where it was good, because much of it was stolen, the rest, buried and stuff that is real was dragged into religion. Names were changed and intergraded into a new version of history. The unresolved, unexplained past, no closure, zero solutions and a continuous battle, as history repeats itself until changed, this can destroy the man in the present, mentally and emotionally. History can wipe you out!

But there's a name for that stuff that breaks a person down to their core. It's called Irish Endurance – and it's a rare gene only found within the

DNA of the Irish person – passed on from our Celtic ancestors. It's a rarity within the world. One must be born and survived in Ireland to inherit such a skill.

But without the solution and answers what we see around us in Ireland is many legends taken by suicide, as the only option, as the way out of this hopelessness. In 2001 – 642 Legends passed on. The Celtic Tiger year – 580 Legends passed on. Every year we're loosing about 500 Legends, in 2009 – 552 people taken by suicide. The pain of the past is wiping out our Legends in the present.

Another Perspective

Let's look at Muslim people for another perspective on all of this, a mainly peaceful religion. The last thing we need is any sort of civil war. These Muslims have been attacked, bombed, their kid's limbs ripped off their bodies, land taken, oil is taken, currency taken and replaced with paper money controlled by the same people who have butchered them, the same Elite. The Muslims who are killing and de-capping are mercenaries hired by the Elite to start off a war, weapons sold to both sides and rage fuelled from all angles. The problem is, some of the victims want to fight back and support this and why wouldn't they? Many of the Muslim people outside the middle east, see what's happening outside Plato's cave and they set up large peaceful group meditations, demonstrating to the world that they are a peaceful people. But the younger men are the resistance of these bombings and attacks; they are joining the mercenaries in a desperate attempt to get some peace for their kid's lives. But they're not sure, who to fight, as it's challenging to find the people behind the scenes pulling the Strings and their last option is to fight the people who support these corrupt governments.

Waves of Muslims on route, with a passion for retaliation, and the controlled media is getting it all going. Can you see this? Its a divide and conquer operation. Once there are kayos in each country in Europe, the American power will be invited into help fix the mess. You remember our King of Leinster did that? And we still haven't recovered. So, don't fall for the player's manipulation of the game. Awareness is the Key.

Now its the 21st Century genocide operation that's happening. It's working because it's keeping us disconnected from our wisdom within, due to the Fluoride in the water, cancer chemicals in the food, chemo for the cancer victims to take all our money and wipe us out. 'With cancer, we're aware they can change the DNA, clone animals and people, and no cure for cancer - you really believe that?

The Queen sends her Love – said she'll hand out a Pillow for the Irish Race to lay its head down and die out. But we're not going to Oblige!

They say, the Queen owns all the gaslights in Ireland. Gas-lighting is a form of manipulation to make a person or group of people believe they are going crazy. Why?

Queen Story

Because… Let's just have a quick look, at the Queen story as it's come to light with DNA testing. An interesting story, not worth much attention but worth a read anyways. The monarchy depends entirely on blood and inheritance.

In the old days, Edward the 4th was King. In 1441 England was at war with France and the Queen of England had a fling with a humble archer. Nine months later Edward was born. Edward is not on the bloodline – not legitimate. The fact is Edward was a bastard child. The King was in France when the Queen got pregnant. 28-April-1442, they tried to pretend it was an 11-month pregnancy. There were a lot of rumours about this at the time. In fact, Edward the 3rd was the last King of England; he was around the time of the War of the Roses.

If the pure bloodline of England occurred and history rewrote itself – we wouldn't have had Henry the 8th. What would England and Ireland have been like if the alternative history happened?

No Henry 8th – so England most likely still be a Catholic country like Ireland, no genocides would have occured. During the circus show of the Royal family, since Edward the 3rd, the new, unimproved royal family is not just a ruthless criminal gang but who's enormous wealth (built on the sufferings of millions) remains a state secret to this day. Beneath the palace gates lies a hidden world of sex scandals, Nazis, murder and even cannibalism. With Queen Elizabeth, the 2nd, all states, Australia, Canada, and the UK swear allegiance not to the people who elected them but to the Queen – including judges, lawyers, and police. Northern Ireland, Canada, and Australia (at times) are still under the Crown, and the Diamond of the crown hat is stolen from India. And just to polish this current state of affairs off....

When you look it up, the Queen owns 600 million pounds, but in reality, her net worth is in the trillions due to ownership of parts of many countries. One investigator said she holds 8.1 Billion Pounds.

Did you know, Brits grew opium poppies in India? They processed it in factories on a colossal scale. Shipped to China and sold to smugglers. 13% of income from India under British rule came from Bengal opium to British run opium distributors in China. Thousands of people branded like cattle as work slaves by the Queen, the hot red steal brand, burnt into people was called DY for Duke of York.

The people of China were in ruin on Opium, and in 1839 the Chinese Emperor said enough! He ordered it all to be seized and destroyed. The opium wars began. It was a ship fight, battleships sent in from Britain with the usual overkill, and the Chinese lost the battle, surrendered and left with no choice but to open five ports to British trade.

Queen now owns 32 trillion dollars. She owns chains of shops and lands all over the world, she owns streets in Manhattan, has an underground getaway, 1 mile deep in the States.

With the Queen structure – they are just looking after their own assets – not the people – the game strategy is plain and straightforward – crown assets are all that matters to them, and their coat of arms says it all – the Lion.

If there is a man-lion and the female lion and they have cub lions. If another man-lion comes along, he kills the father lion, and he eats the cubs and starts again.

And were back to, he who has the Gold – makes the Rules.
Australia has no Gold – it did have but was taken out, handed to the Bank of England – buried in Volts under the Themes – Thread Needle street. If people get past the security – they can flood it. Gold and Silver are the only valuable currencies on the planet.

Whoever has the Gold - makes the rules!

'We have been trapped in a Triangle for centuries - the triangle consists of Persecutor (Queen Establishment) - Rescuer (Pope Establishment) and Victim (Ireland).

"They must find it difficult...
those who have taken authority as truth rather than truth as authority."

But as you can see, The Irish Celts are made of Endurance and Resilience! Look what we have been subjected to and still we Rise and Rise as the Irish legends, loved and respected, for our fight for a better future, for our resilience, for our love and compassion towards all human beings, and for our creativity and our education around the world.

Be proud troops, be very proud!

CHAPTER 12

It's the 21ˢᵗ Century

DNA is life and a record holder. When you see DNA up close, it's like looking at a Universe, as there is so much data in it, that records a true history of us all the way back to what they call the Big Bang, the start of existence.

If we look into DNA, everyone's is different, unique, but we are all part of the same code of DNA on this planet Earth, it is all one code of DNA, from a fish to a bird, to a wolf and to a person.

Those in power, the real power, the influencers of war, of invasions, media influencers, government godfathers and mafias are working hard to ingrain systems that separate us through race, religion, sexuality, health, for the divide and conquer strategy of domination.

The human race has been suppressed through various systems and the rising needed to challenge these systems are becoming a reality - but this is our story of Èire and the Awakening of the Celt.

We have designed and built much of this material world - we have civilized the western world, we have influenced much of the world with political involvement, we were neutral in world wars, peace keepers in war torn zones. We are known for singing songs with such passion and by having the Craic everywhere we go. We are good entertainers, always telling funny stories, teaching skills and giving education to people throughout the globe. The Irish are a foundation for many of the worlds history today and our influence in the global village of today is phenomenal in every regard.

We have been trapped in a triangle for a 1000 years. The triangle involved Ireland and two Empires. The triangle consists of Persecutor, Rescuer and Victim. We have been in the Victim position for generations and we now need to rise above Victimhood.

The solution for the conflict/drama triangle is to change the Persecutor to Challenger, The Rescuer to a Life Saver and the Victim to Creator!

Ireland's solution for the 21st century is to fulfill Dev's 1937 Constitution which states, all of Ireland, - its islands and oceans should be owned and run by the Irish people. Irish Ownership & Land Rights!

We are the Awakening of the Celt.

So, we had a few minor distractions, (minor set backs) and a few interruptions over the centuries - lets get back to the intentions we had when our ancestors built New Grange - An Awakening!

Regarding our true culture - as per the cover of this book, we have three bright stars known as Orion's Belt. The stars are called now as they always were - The 3 Kings and they point towards the North Star - all towards the Birth of the Sun as it Rises once again lighting up our New Grange Celtic Cross.

(The foundation - the real story behind many religious stories throughout the globe)

We are a 3 part being.
What you think - you become.

What you feel - you attract.
What you imagine - you create.

The swirls on the Rock at New Grange entrance is in symbolism of the 3 part individual. It's a welcoming entrance - saying Welcome to the Awakening. We are made up of mind, body and consciousness. The White Quartz Rock gives off a vibration to help connect us to source, our consciousness within.

The entrance to New Grange is 19 meters long with 3 recesses. Our Celtic Cross is our pathway to moving up the levels of growth and becoming Self-Realized as the gods we were born to be.

We are a 3 part being with 7 Celtic knots and when we respond too each other from all 3 parts and all 7 centers in the same moment, then we have reached the peak experience of our very existence!

We had an amazing civilization in Ireland that consisted of 37 amazing structures in Slane, around New Grange and our High Kings used the Hill of Tara for the Celebrations of the Birth of the Sun.

It's all still there! The building of New Grange was to be an Awakening to Authentic Purpose - to take us to the next level & levels beyond!

We Are The Awakening Of The Celt!

Trilogy

CPSIA information can be obtained
at www.ICGtesting.com
Printed in the USA
BVHW030813150319
542770BV00005B/19/P